The Best of Success

A TREASURY OF INSPIRATION

Mac Anderson & Bob Kelly

Copyright © 2009 by Simple Truths
Published by Simple Truths
1952 McDowell Road, Suite 205
Naperville, Illinois 60563

Book Design: Brian Frantz

Simple Truths is a registered trademark.
Printed in China.
ISBN 978-1-60810-063-7

www.simpletruths.com
Toll Free 800-900-3427

Photo Credits:
Fotolia : Title Page, Page Backgrounds, 6, 31, 36, 66, 78, 84, 90, 102, 138, 144
IStock : Back Cover, 12, 48, 54, 60, 66, 72, 96, 108, 114, 120, 126
Ken Jenkins : 18
Todd Reed : Cover

02 4CPG 12

Table of Contents

Table of Contents

Introduction

Success! Such a magical word like gold or love or Shangri-la, it conjures up different but always enticing visions in the minds of all of us.

\- Og Mandino

*S*uccess! A magical word indeed, but what exactly is it? A one-time thing, like hitting a home run, scoring a touchdown, or winning a game? Is it a destination? Or a journey? Is there a fixed, clearly marked place called "Success"? Or does it vary from individual to individual?

Does success mean achievement, or fame, or power, or wealth? Who decides when one has become "successful"? Can it be self-conferred? Is it, like beauty, in the eye of the beholder? Can we objectively define it? Or is it a relative thing? Can two people have nearly identical track records and yet one be seen as successful and the other to have failed?

Is success a specific target to aim at, like making a million dollars or becoming the CEO of a large corporation? Can it be clearly seen by everyone?

Down through the ages, thousands of people have asked similar questions, and thousands more have suggested answers. For example, for the famous Greek philosopher Aristotle (384-322 B.C.), it was a life of service. Two centuries earlier, the Chinese philosopher Confucius (551-479 B.C.) declared that the key to success was preparation. For 18th century Anglo-Irish poet Oliver Goldsmith, success meant "getting up just one more time than you fall." And Benjamin Franklin advised that success required "jumping quickly at opportunities."

In his book, *Success Is a Moving Target* (Word Books, 1975), author Robert A. Raines asked: "What is success for you? Where is the target moving for you? Do you feel an inner tug, pull, nudge, ache, some sense that it's getting away from you again?"

In our research for this book, it became very clear that defining and describing success is no easy task. It is indeed a moving target, as subjective as it is elusive. Yet, there are traits which many of those we consider successful seem to share, and identifying at least some of them is what this book is all about. We hope the quotations about them, and the stories behind each of them, will be a source of inspiration in your journey along the highway to success.

Never mind what others do;
do better than yourself,
beat your own record from day to day,
and you are a success.

- William J.H. Boetcker

Believe in Yourself

She was born to Jewish parents in Russia in 1898. When she was eight years old, her family moved to the United States, settling in Milwaukee. Her parents enrolled her in a local school, although she knew no English. Nevertheless, by the time she graduated, she was valedictorian of her class.

In 1921, she and her husband moved to Palestine and she soon became actively involved in Zionist politics. Because of her leadership abilities, she was given increasingly important assignments. In 1948, as the time drew near the establishment of the nation of Israel, she traveled to the United States, where she raised $50 million for the cause of independence.

After serving as Minister of Labour in the new government, and then Foreign Minister, she retired from public life in 1966 due to ill health. However, in 1969, she became Israel's Prime Minister, the first woman to hold that post, where she served with great distinction for five years.

Golda Meir had come a long way from her humble beginning in Russia to leadership of a nation. She once summed up her "secret of success" in these words: "Trust yourself. Create the kind of self that you will be happy to live with all your life. Make the most of yourself by fanning the tiny, inner sparks of possibility into flames of achievement."

There are many roads one can travel toward success, some smooth, others filled with potholes and detours, but, as Golda Meir so eloquently reminds us, each has the same starting point – oneself!

Don't limit yourself.
Many people limit themselves to what they **think** they can do.
You can go as far as your mind lets you.
What you **believe**, remember, you can achieve.
- Mary Kay Ash

Until you make room in your life

for someone as important to you as **yourself**,
you will always be searching and lost.
- Richard Bach

Your **success** depends mainly upon what you think of yourself

and whether you **believe** in yourself.
You can succeed if nobody else believes it;
but you will never succeed if you don't believe in yourself.
- William J.H. Boetcker

All the **wonders** you seek are within yourself.
- Thomas Brown

There is only one way in the world to be **distinguished**.
Follow your instinct!
Be **yourself**, and you'll be somebody.
- Bliss Carman

Trust yourself. Think for yourself.
Act for yourself. Speak for yourself.
Be yourself.
Imitation is suicide.
- Marva Collins

To be yourself in a world that is constantly trying
to make you something else is the **greatest** accomplishment.
- Ralph Waldo Emerson

Don't bother just to be better than your contemporaries or
predecessors.
Try to **be better** than yourself.
- William Faulkner

One must have the **adventurous** daring to accept oneself
as a bundle of possibilities and undertake the most
interesting game in the world – making the most of one's **best**.
- Harry Emerson Fosdick

Be a **first rate** version of yourself,
not a second rate version of someone else.
- Judy Garland

Be **yourself**.
Who else is better qualified?
- *Frank Giblin II*

What another would have done as well as you, do not do it.
What another would have said as well as you, do not say it.
What another would have written as well, do not write it.
Be **faithful** to that which exists nowhere but in yourself.
- *André Gide*

The most **important** person to listen to is oneself,
and our most important task is to develop an ear
that can really **hear** what we are saying.
- *Sydney J. Harris*

You need to **feel good** about yourself,
the motivation has to come from within.
You have nobody to fall back on except yourself.
- *Dana Hill*

There's only one corner of the universe you can
be certain of **improving** and that's your own self.
- *Aldous Huxley*

**Never underestimate yourself.
You are the most important thing in your universe.**
- Edward L. Kramer

If you want to be truly successful, invest in yourself to
get the **knowledge** you need to find your unique factor.
When you find it and focus on it and persevere,
your success will **blossom**.
- Sydney Madwed

The picture you have of yourself, your **self-esteem**,
will have a profound effect on the way you see the world
and the way your world sees you.
- Earl Nightingale

People become really quite **remarkable** when they
start thinking that they can do things.
When they **believe** in themselves they have the first secret of success.
- Norman Vincent Peale

Self-reliance is the only road to true **freedom**,
and being one's own person is its ultimate reward.
- Patricia Sampson

So you've got a problem? That's good! Why?
Because repeated victories over your
problems are the rungs
on your ladder to success.
With each victory you grow in
wisdom, stature and experience.
You become a bigger,
better, more successful
person each time you meet
a problem
and tackle and conquer it with a
positive mental attitude.

- W. Clement Stone

Have a Positive Attitude

W. Clement Stone was a successful businessman, author and philanthropist. A strong proponent of the power of attitude, he first gained fame in 1960 as the co-author, with Napoleon Hill, of *Success Through a Positive Mental Attitude*. During a lifetime that spanned a century, he continued to champion the philosophy that the right attitude could overcome virtually every problem.

Norman Cousins had problems, primarily health related, which had affected him for much of his life. A journalist and editor, he began his career as a book critic for a magazine and soon became managing editor. In 1940, he joined *Saturday Review of Literature* and, two years later, was named editor-in-chief. During his 30 years in that position, circulation increased from 20,000 to 650,000.

At one point, Cousins became seriously ill and was diagnosed with a degenerative inflammatory disease which caused him considerable pain. He also suffered from heart disease, and doctors gave him little chance of survival. But Cousins was a firm believer in the power of a positive attitude, and refused to accept as fact the prognosis he'd received. "Optimism doesn't wait on facts," he said. "It deals with prospects. Pessimism is a waste of time."

Cousins checked himself out of the hospital and into a nearby hotel room, where he self-prescribed megadoses of Vitamin C and – laughter! He began watching old Marx Brothers films, over and over. The result: "I made the joyous discovery that ten minutes of genuine belly laughter had an anesthetic effect and would give me at least two hours of pain-free sleep."

Short-term relief is one thing, but did Cousins' positive mental attitude have any long-range benefits? Considering the fact that he lived for 16 productive and successful years beyond what his doctors predicted, the answer is clearly "Yes!"

Attitude is the mind's **paintbrush**.
It can color a situation gloomy or gray, or cheerful…
In fact, attitudes are more important than facts.
- *Mary C. Crowley*

If you don't like something, **change it**.
If you can't change it, change your attitude. Don't complain.
- *Maya Angelou*

Our attitudes control our lives. Attitudes are a **secret power** working
twenty-four hours a day, for good or bad. It is of paramount importance that we
know how to harness and control this **great** force.
- *Tom Blandi*

The **worth** of a man is revealed in his attitude to ordinary things
when he is not before the **footlights**.
- *Oswald Chambers*

Ability is what you're capable of doing. **Motivation** determines what you do.
Attitude determines how well you do it.
- *Raymond Chandler*

Our success or our failure is the result of our **mental** condition
– our thoughts about people and about ourselves
– our attitudes toward people and toward ourselves.
- Dan Custer

Your living is determined not so much by what **life** brings to you as by the attitude you bring to life; not so much by what happens to you as by the way your **mind** looks at what happens.
- Kahlil Gibran

Preserve a right mental attitude – the attitude of **courage**, frankness and good cheer. To think rightly is to **create**.
- Elbert Hubbard

A great attitude is not the result of SUCCESS; success is the result of a great attitude.
- Earl Nightingale

Nothing can stop the man with the **right** mental attitude from achieving his goal; **nothing** on earth can help the man with the wrong mental attitude.
- Thomas Jefferson

Could we change our **attitude**, we should not only see life differently, but life itself would come to be different. Life would undergo a change of appearance because we ourselves had undergone a change of **attitude**.
- *Katherine Mansfield*

Your living is determined not so much by what **life** brings to you as by the attitude you bring to life; not so much by what happens to you as by the way your mind looks at what happens. **Circumstances** and **situations** do color life, but you have been given the mind to choose what the color shall be.
- *John Homer Miller*

A strong **positive** mental attitude will create
more **miracles** than any wonder drug.
- *Patricia Neal*

Any fact facing us is not as important as our attitude toward it, for that determines our **success** or failure.
- *Norman Vincent Peale*

Success is ninety-nine per cent **mental attitude**. It calls for love, joy, optimism, confidence, serenity, poise, faith, courage, cheerfulness, imagination, initiative, tolerance, honesty, humility, patience and enthusiasm.
- *Wilferd A. Peterson*

The **meanings** of things lies not in the things themselves
but in our attitude towards them.
- Antoine de Saint-Exupéry

Eagles come in all shapes and sizes, but you will **recognize** them
chiefly by their **attitudes**.
- Charles Prestwich Scott

There is little difference in people, but that little difference makes a
big difference. The little difference is attitude. The big **difference** is
whether it is **positive** or negative.
- W. Clement Stone

The point of living, and of being an **optimist**,
is to be foolish enough to believe the **best** is yet to come.
- Peter Ustinov

It is not your aptitude, but your **attitude**,
that determines your **altitude**.
- Zig Ziglar

The character that takes command in moments of crucial choices has already been determined by... the little choices of years past — by all those times when the voice of conscience was at war with the voice of temptation, whispering the lie that "it really doesn't matter".

- Ronald Reagan

Make Integrity Your Watchword

*I*n the world of tennis, Eliot Teltscher never became as famous as Jimmy Connors or John McEnroe. Yet, during his professional career, from 1977 to 1988, he was consistently ranked among the world's top ten players, winning 10 singles titles and more than $1.6 million in prize money.

Teltscher began playing tennis at age nine. After high school, he received a tennis scholarship to UCLA, and was named an All-American as a freshman. Then he left college to turn professional. In 1982, he was ranked #6 in the world. He retired as a player in 1988, and currently serves as a National Coach for the United States Tennis Association.

But, despite his many accomplishments, when asked about the highlights of his career, the first thing he usually mentions isn't about victories or awards. Instead, he describes a match he lost, but which speaks volumes about him.

In January 1982, playing Vitas Gerulaitis, also a Top-10 player, the latter was at match point in the final set. His last shot barely cleared the net, seemingly out of Teltscher's reach but, somehow, he got his racket on the ball and lofted it over his opponent's head, winning the point.

There was a problem, however, which neither Gerulaitis nor the umpire, nor anyone else realized. But Teltscher did – and nothing else mattered. In rushing for that final shot, his racket had barely grazed the net, which violated the rules. Without hesitation, he informed the umpire, costing him the point and the match.

B.C. Forbes, who founded *Forbes* magazine nearly a century ago, once commented that "Integrity is the basis of all true-blue success." For Eliot Teltscher, he faced a moment when his integrity and his character were at stake, and that was far more important than winning a tennis match. In defeat, he achieved not only a real victory but "true-blue success."

Let **unswerving** integrity ever be your watchword.
- Bernard M. Baruch

A **successful life** is not an easy life. It is built upon strong qualities, sacrifice, endeavor, loyalty, integrity.
- Grant D. Brandon

Integrity has no need of rules.
- Albert Camus

Nothing so completely baffles one who is full of trick and duplicity himself, than **straightforward** and **simple** integrity in another.
- Charles Caleb Colton

I am for integrity, if only because life is very short and **truth** is hard to come by.
- Kermit Eby

Nothing is at last sacred but the integrity of **your** own **mind**.
- Ralph Waldo Emerson

Integrity is the **essence** of everything successful.
- R. Buckminster Fuller

Men of integrity, by their very existence, rekindle the **belief** that as a people we can live above the level of moral squalor.
- John W. Gardner

The integrity of men is to be **measured** by their **conduct**, not by their professions.
- Junius

Integrity is one of several paths. It **distinguishes itself** from the others because it is the right path and the only one on which you will never get lost.
- M.H. McKee

Once you lose your **enthusiasm**, you lose your integrity.
And once you lose your **integrity**, you're a con man.
- Russ Reid

I would rather be the man who **bought** the Brooklyn Bridge
than the man who sold it.
- Will Rogers

Don't worry so much about your **self-esteem**.
Worry more about your **character**. Integrity is its own reward.
- Dr. Laura Schlessinger

**Better keep yourself clean and bright;
you are the window through which you must see the world.**
- George Bernard Shaw

Integrity is the first step to true **greatness**. Men love to praise, but are slow to
practice it. To maintain it in high places costs self-denial; in all places it is liable to
opposition, but its end is **glorious**, and the universe will yet do it homage.
- Charles Simmons

If you have **integrity**, nothing else matters.
If you don't have **integrity**, nothing else matters.
- Alan K. Simpson

**Society is built upon trust and trust upon confidence
in one another s integrity.**
- Robert South

Give us the man of integrity, on whom we know we can thoroughly **depend**;
who will stand firm when others fail; the friend, faithful and true; the adviser,
honest and **fearless**; the adversary, just and chivalrous,
such a one is a fragment of the Rock of Ages.
- A.P. Stanley

A man, after he has brushed off the dust and chips of his life,
will have left only the hard, clean question:
Was it **good** or was it evil? Have I done **well** – or ill?
- John Steinbeck

A life lived with integrity – even if it lacks the trappings of fame and fortune –
is a **shining star** in whose light others may follow in the years to come.
- Denis Waitley

There are some people who live in a dream world, and there are some who face reality; and then there are those who turn one into the other.

- Desiderius Erasmus

Realize Your Dreams

"*You*'re living in a dream world" is typically meant as criticism. It suggests the recipient is out of touch with reality, or incompetent. But let's take another look at that statement.

First of all, dreams have motivated countless millions to begin the journey along the highway to success. As the following story shows, a dream world can be a good place to live – as long as we don't become permanent residents.

In June 1940, a 4½-pound baby girl was born to a poor family in rural and segregated Tennessee. The 20th of 22 children, she was sickly, contracting one illness after another. At age 4, she developed lameness in her left foot and leg, and was diagnosed with polio, which was then incurable. It seemed she was destined to spend her life in leg braces.

The only nearby hospital was for whites only so, twice a week, her mother drove her 50 miles for treatment. Those long road trips gave the child time to dream, as she visualized what her life could be like without braces.

Wilma Rudolph had no intention of staying in her dream world. By age 12, with constant exercise, she had shed her braces. She could walk on her own – and she could run! Oh, how she could run! She earned a track scholarship to college and, in 1960, at the Summer Olympic Games in Rome, she became the first American woman ever to win three gold medals in Olympic competition.

After returning from Rome, and until her death from cancer in 1994, she enjoyed a distinguished career as a teacher, coach, broadcaster and founder of the Wilma Rudolph Foundation. No longer living in her dream world, she was quick to acknowledge the value of the time she spent there. "Never underestimate the power of dreams and the influence of the human spirit," she said. "The potential for greatness lies within each of us."

The key to **happiness** is having **dreams**;
the key to success is making them come true.
- James Lane Allen

Dreams do come true, if we only **wish** hard enough.
You can have **anything** in life if you will sacrifice everything else for it.
- James M. Barrie

**All our dreams can come true
if we have the courage to pursue them.**
- Walt Disney

To dream anything that you want to dream,
That is the **beauty** of the human mind.
To do anything that you want to do,
That is the strength of the human will.
To **trust** yourself to test your limits,
That is the courage to succeed.
- Bernard Edmonds

I am a **dreamer**. I am, indeed, a practical dreamer.
My dreams are not airy nothings.
I want to convert my dreams into realities, as far as possible.
- Mohandas K. Gandhi

Behind every advance of the human race is a germ of **creation** growing in the mind of some lone individual – an individual whose **dreams** waken him in the night while others lie contentedly asleep.
- Crawford H. Greenewalt

Cherish your **visions** and your dreams, as they are the children of your **soul**, the blueprints of your ultimate accomplishments.
- Napoleon Hill

Dreamers are the architects of **greatness**. Their brains have wrought all human miracles... They are the chosen few – the blazers of the way – who never wear doubt's bandage on their eyes.
- Herbert Kaufman

Dreams are extremely important. You can't do it unless you imagine it.
- George Lucas

Do you believe in **dreams**? Don't oversleep if you want your dreams to come true! Don't let dreams become nightmares.
- Henrietta C. Mears

A steadfast **soul**, holding steadily to a dream ideal,
plus a sturdy will determined to **succeed** in any venture,
can make any dream come true.
- B.N. Mills

To achieve anything **significant**,
everyone needs a little **imagination** and a big dream.
- Norman Vincent Peale

They who dream by day are cognizant of many things
which **escape** those who dream only by night.
- Edgar Allen Poe

Dreams grow holy put in **action**.
- Adelaide Anne Procter

**There are no limits to growth and human progress when
men and women are free to follow their dreams.**
- Ronald Reagan

Your hopes, dreams and **aspirations** are legitimate.
They are trying to take you airborne, above the storms,
above the clouds – if you will only let them.
- Diane Roger

Nothing happens unless **first** a dream.
- Carl Sandburg

If one advances **confidently** in the direction of his dreams, and endeavors to
live the life which he has imagined, he will meet with a
success unexpected in common hours.
- Henry David Thoreau

If you have built castles in the air, your work need not be lost; that is where they
should be. Now put **foundations** under them.
- Henry David Thoreau

When we dare to dream, many **marvels** can be accomplished.
The trouble is, most people never start dreaming their impossible dream.
- Glenn Van Ekeren

A vision foretells
what may be ours. It is an
invitation to do something. With
a great mental picture in mind
we go from one accomplishment to another.

- Katherine Logan

Try Something New

*T*he year was 1936. On a hot summer afternoon in a small South Dakota town, Dorothy Hustead lay down for a nap with her two little children. But the noise from the jalopies chugging by outside her window kept her awake, and it was then that she had a vision. No, it wasn't an apparition or some sort of mystical experience. It was far more practical than that; it was a vision that was destined to have an enormous impact on the Hustead family, their struggling business, and their little town – an impact that continues to this day.

Dorothy thought about the people in those cars and how hot and thirsty they must have been as they drove along in the blistering hot prairie sun. She rushed to share her vision with her husband Ted, a pharmacist who was struggling to make a living in the small drugstore they had purchased five years earlier. Lots of cars passed by their store every day, but very few stopped.

Dorothy suggested putting up a few signs along nearby highways, offering free ice water to everyone who visited their store. Today, thousands of Wall Drug signs stretch across America, still announcing the free ice water Dorothy envisioned long ago. As a direct result of her vision, as many as 20,000 people from all over the world visit every day.

Far more than a drug store, Wall Drug is now a 76,000-square-foot western tourist attraction, still run by members of the Hustead family. The sprawling enterprise specializes in western items, Native American artifacts, fine art, decorative accessories, food and drink, and gifts and collectibles. There's also a spacious restaurant, a traveler's chapel and a play area for children. And, yes, the ice water is still free.

The story of Wall Drug is a typical American success story, built on the vision of a young wife and mother more than seventy years ago.

The **vision** that you glorify in your mind, the **ideal** that you enthrone in your heart – this you will build your life by, this you will become.
- James Lane Allen

Be daring, be different, be impractical; be anything that will assert **integrity** of purpose and imaginative **vision** against the play-it-safers, the creatures of the commonplace, the slaves of the ordinary.
- Cecil Beaton

The secret of making something work in your lives is, first of all, the deep **desire** to make it work: then the faith and **belief** that it can work: then to hold that clear definite vision in your consciousness and see it working out step by step, without one thought of doubt or disbelief.
- Eileen Caddy

Vision: it reaches beyond the thing that is, into the conception of what can be. **Imagination** gives you the picture.
Vision gives you the impulse to make the picture your own.
- Robert Collier

If you have a **VISION**, do something with it.
- Anthony J. D'Angelo

I prefer to be a **dreamer** among the humblest, with visions to be realized, than lord among those without dreams and **desires**.
- Kahlil Gibran

Never look down to test the ground before taking your next step; only he who keeps his eyes fixed on the far horizon will find the **right** road.
- Dag Hammarskjöld

The vision must be followed by the venture. It is not enough to stare up the steps we must step up the stairs.
- Vance Havner

A blind man's world is bounded by the limits of his **touch**; an ignorant man's world by the limits of his **knowledge**; a great man's world by the limits of his **vision**.
- E. Paul Hovey

Your vision will become **clear** only when you look into your **heart**. Who looks outside, dreams; who looks inside, awakens.
- Carl Jung

Two men look out through the same bars:
One sees the mud, and one the **stars**.
- Frederick Langbridge

Aim for a star, and keep your sights high! With a heart full of **faith** within, your feet on the ground and your eyes in the sky.
- Helen Lowrie Marshall

Throughout the centuries there were men who took first steps down new roads armed with nothing but their own VISION.
- Ayn Rand

Visionary people are **visionary** partly because of the very great many things they don't **see**.
- Berkeley Rice

The balanced man is he whose **thoughts** soar on the wings of vision – but whose feet remain on the rocks of **reality**.
- J.A. Rosenkranz

A rock pile ceases to be a rock pile the moment a single man
contemplates it, bearing within him the image of a cathedral.
- Antoine de Saint-Exupéry

**Every great work, every big accomplishment, has been brought into
manifestation through holding to the vision.**
- Florence Scovel Shinn

Vision without a task is only a **dream**. A task without a vision is but drudgery.
But vision with a task is a dream fulfilled.
- Willie Stone

True **originality** consists not in a new manner but in a new vision.
- Edith Wharton

The seed, or germ, of all **successful** effort is in a trained imagination.
If you can't picture your goal, you won't have the **courage** to start.
Your imagination is working with you or against you every minute of
every hour of every week of every year of your life.
- A.B. ZuTavern

Each golden sunrise ushers in new opportunities for those who retain faith in themselves, and keep their chins up. No one has ever seen a cock crow with its head down... Meet the sunrise with confidence.

- Alonzo Newton Benn

Have Faith in Yourself

Mary Kathlyn Wagner was born in the little Texas town of Hot Wells in 1918. Married at age 17, she soon had three children. When her husband was called to war, she supported her family by selling books door to door. After his return, they were divorced and she went to work for a local company, becoming a sales director. After 25 years, she quit, when yet another man she had trained was promoted above her, at twice what she was making.

In her mid-forties by then, she had no intention of giving up. As a child, she'd been told again and again by her mother: "You can do it! You can do it!" That faith, that belief in herself, that level of confidence her mother had instilled in her would serve her well. Using her life savings of $5,000 and enlisting the help of her 20-year-old son, she opened a small store in Dallas, catering to women's beauty needs.

That was the modest beginning of what would become a huge international company, with more than 1.8 million Independent Beauty Consultants selling the products of Mary Kay Inc. all around the world.

Mary Kay Ash never forgot the lesson her mother taught her. One of her favorite sayings was: "Aerodynamically, the bumble bee shouldn't be able to fly, but the bumble bee doesn't know it, so it goes on flying anyway."

So Mary Kay kept right on flying, and helping countless numbers of women achieve a level of success they might have otherwise only dreamed about. To those who sought to climb the ladder of success, she offered this advice: "Don't limit yourself. Many people limit themselves to what they think they can do. You can go as far as your mind lets you. What you believe, remember, you can achieve."

Nothing splendid has ever been achieved except by those who dared **believe** that something inside them was superior to circumstance.
- Bruce Barton

Your success depends mainly upon what you **think** of yourself and whether you believe in yourself. You can **succeed** if nobody else believes it; but you will never succeed if you don't believe in yourself.
- William J.H. Boetcker

Confidence is that feeling by which the mind embarks in great and honorable courses with a sure hope and trust in itself.
- Cicero

The only thing that stands between a man and what he wants from **life** is often merely the will to try it and the **faith** to believe that it is possible.
- Richard M. DeVos

Faith is not trying to **believe** something regardless of the evidence:
Faith is **daring** to do something regardless of the consequences.
- Sherwood Eddy

Success is not what you think it is... it is what you believe it is.
- *Doug Firebaugh*

Don't aim for success if you want it; just do what you **love** and **believe** in, and it will come naturally.
- *David Frost*

I have lived eighty-six years. I have watched men **climb up** to success, hundreds of them, and of all the elements that are important for success, the most important is **faith**. No great thing comes to any man unless he has **courage**.
- *Cardinal James Gibbons*

Faith is the bird that feels the **light** and sings to greet the dawn while it is still dark.
- *James S. Hewett*

Whatever the mind can conceive and **believe**, the mind can **achieve**.
- *Napoleon Hill*

Believe. No pessimist ever discovered the **secrets** of the stars,
or sailed to an uncharted land, or opened a new heaven to the human **spirit**.
- Helen Keller

I will forget the happenings of the day that is gone,
where they were **good** or bad, and greet the new sun with confidence
that this will be the **best** day of my life.
- Og Mandino

Fear of failure and fear of the unknown are always defeated by **faith**.
Having faith in yourself, in the process of change, and in the new direction
that change sets will reveal your own inner **core** of steel.
- Georgette Mosbacher

**Confidence is like going after Moby Dick with a rowboat,
a harpoon and a jar of tartar sauce.**
- Robert Orben

People become really quite **remarkable** when they start thinking
that they can do things. When they believe in themselves,
they have the first secret of success.
- Norman Vincent Peale

Faith is an **excitement** and an **enthusiasm**: it is a condition of intellectual magnificence to which we must cling as to a treasure.
- *George Sand*

Confidence doesn't come out of nowhere. It's a result of something: hours and days and weeks and years of constant work and dedication.
- *Roger Staubach*

Faith in your own powers and **confidence** in your individual methods are essential to success.
- *Roderick Stevens*

If one advances confidently in the direction of his **dreams**, and endeavors to live the life which he has imagined,

he will meet with a **success** unexpected in common hours.
- *Henry David Thoreau*

Confidence! Confidence! **Confidence**! That is your capital.
- *John Wanamaker*

The man who grasps an opportunity as it is paraded before him, nine times out of ten makes a success; but the man who makes his own opportunities is, barring an accident, a sure-fire success.

- Dale Carnegie

Opportunity Awaits You

Russell Conwell was born in Massachusetts in 1843. During the Civil War, he was a Captain in the Union Army, and then became a lawyer and a writer. In 1879, he began studying for the ministry and, in 1882, became pastor of a new Baptist church in Philadelphia which, under his leadership, would become that city's world-renowned Baptist Temple. In 1887, he founded Temple University, and was named president, a post he would hold until his death in 1925.

Conwell's distinguished service as a pastor and educator brought him many honors, but his greatest success came as a result of a legend he had heard in 1870, while on a round-the-world journey, representing a Boston-based travel publication. One day, his guide told him the ancient tale of a Persian farmer named Ali Hafed who, dreaming of great riches, had sold his land to go in search of diamonds. But, after searching in vain for years, his health and his money gone, he cast himself into the sea and drowned.

Meanwhile, the man to whom Ali Hafed had sold his property found a small stone in the shallow brook on his newly purchased land. It was a diamond, the first of thousands in what would prove to be, in the words of Conwell's guide, "the most magnificent diamond mine in all the history of mankind."

That Persian legend became the theme of a speech Conwell would deliver more than 6,000 times. Titled "Acres of Diamonds," it was also published in book form, becoming one of the most famous books ever published.

Conwell's message is as valid a formula for success today as it was a century ago: "Your diamonds are not in far distant mountains or in yonder seas; they are in your own backyard if you but dig for them."

Look sharply and you will see **opportunity**;
for though she is blind, she is not invisible.
- Francis Bacon

What is the difference between an obstacle and an opportunity?
Our **attitude** toward it. Every opportunity has a difficulty,
and every difficulty has an opportunity.
- J. Sidlow Baxter

When one door closes, another opens; but we often **look** so long and
so regretfully upon the closed door that we do not see
the one which has **opened** for us.
- Alexander Graham Bell

The lure of the distant and the difficult is deceptive.
The **great** opportunity is where you are.
- John Burroughs

The sure way to miss success is to miss the opportunity.
- Victor Charles

The reason so many people never get anywhere in life is because,
when opportunity **knocks**,
they are out in the backyard looking for four-leaf clovers.
- Walter P. Chrysler

The **secret** of **success** in life is for a man to be ready for
his opportunity when it comes.
- Benjamin Disraeli

We are all continually faced with a series of **great** opportunities,
brilliantly disguised as insoluble problems.
- John W. Gardner

To improve the golden moment of opportunity,
and catch the good that is within our reach, is the great art of life.
- Samuel Johnson

The **golden opportunity** you are seeking is in yourself.
It is not in your environment; it is not in luck or chance,
or the help of others; it is in yourself alone.
- Orison Swett Marden

None of us knows what the next **change** is going to be,
what unexpected **opportunity** is just around the corner,
waiting a few months or a few years to change all the tenor of our lives.
- Kathleen Norris

Opportunities should never be lost, because they can hardly be regained.
- William Penn

Vigilance in watching opportunity; tact and daring in seizing upon opportunity;
force and **persistence** in crowding opportunity to its utmost of possible
achievement – these are the martial virtues which must command **success**.
- Austin Phelps

The ladder of **success** is best climbed by stepping on the rungs of opportunity.
- Ayn Rand

The tragedy of many lives is not that our **talents** are few, but that too frequently we do not use the ones **entrusted** to us. We pray for bigger opportunities
but do not make use of the opportunities that lie in our paths.
- Virgil A. Reed

Life's up and downs provide windows of opportunity
to determine your **values** and **goals**.
Think of using all obstacles as stepping stones to build the life you want.
- Marsha Sinetar

Do what you're afraid to do. When you run away because you are
afraid to do something big, you pass **opportunity** by.
- W. Clement Stone

The world is full of **abundance** and opportunity, but far too many people
come to the fountain of **life** with a sieve instead of a tank car ... a teaspoon
instead of a steam shovel. They expect little and as a result they get little.
- Ben Sweetland

There is no security in life, only opportunity.
- Mark Twain

Opportunities are **swarming** around us all the time, thicker than
gnats at sundown. We walk through a cloud of them.
- Henry Van Dyke

Change is the watchword of progression. When we tire of well-worn ways, we seek for new. This restless craving in the souls of men spurs them to climb, and to seek the mountain view.

- Ella Wheeler Wilcox

Greet Change as a Friend

Shortly after taking office in 1977 as President of the United States, Jimmy Carter appointed his friend and fellow Georgian, Bert Lance, as director of the Office of Management and the Budget (OMB).

Before long, investigations began into certain irregularities at a Georgia bank, and of Lance's role as its chairman. With the Watergate scandal still fresh in the minds of many Americans, the media had a field day with Lance, and he soon resigned from his OMB post. Forced to stand trial for his alleged improprieties at his bank, where he had stepped down as chairman, he was later acquitted of all charges, and resumed his leadership role.

Lance would probably have been long forgotten by now, except for one brief comment during a May 1977 interview with *Nation's Business* magazine. Today, that statement, "If it ain't broke, don't fix it," remains the clarion call of the status quo crowd – the NIMBYs (Not In My Back Yard), the NOPEs (Not On Planet Earth) and the BANANAS (Build Absolutely Nothing Anywhere Near Anything). It has taken its place alongside such old bromides as "Don't make waves," and "Leave well enough alone."

Pastor/educator/author C. Neil Strait might well have had the "if it ain't broke" crowd in mind when he wrote: "Change is always hard for the man who is in a rut. For he has scaled down his living to that which he can handle comfortably and welcomes no change – or challenge – that would lift him."

Rather than following the Lance approach, those who seek some measure of success in life might consider these words by the late American philosopher and educator John Dewey: "Since changes are going on anyway, the great thing is to learn enough about them so that we will be able to lay hold of them and turn them in the direction of our desires."

The need for **change** bulldozed a road down the center of my **mind**.
- Maya Angelou

When you're through **changing**, you're through.
- Bruce Barton

Our days are a **kaleidoscope**. Every instant a change takes place in the contents. New harmonies, new contrasts, new combinations of every sort. Nothing ever happens twice alike.
- Henry Ward Beecher

Change is a process and not a destination, it never ends!
- James Belasco

To exist is to change, to change is to mature,
to mature is to go on **creating** oneself endlessly.
- Henri Bergson

We must all obey the **great** law of change.
It is the most powerful law of nature.
- Edmund Burke

Life is change. Growth is optional. Choose wisely.
- Karen Kaiser Clark

Change does not necessarily assure progress,
but **progress** implacably requires change.
- Henry Steele Commager

If you don't like the way the world is, you **change it**.
You have an obligation to change it. You just do it one step at a time.
- Marian Wright Edelman

Little men with little minds and little **imagination** jog through life in little ruts,
smugly resisting all changes which would jar their little worlds.
- Marie Fraser

We need more unreasonable people who want to change the world,
not to adapt to it**...** I believe**...** it is our **responsibility**
to make it better and not just to survive.
- *Charles Handy*

Everything in the universe is subject to change
and everything is right on schedule.
- *Gay Hendricks*

If one is going to **change** things,
one has to make a fuss and catch the eye of the **world**.
- *Elizabeth Janeway*

I cannot say whether things will get **better** if we change;
what I can say is they must change if they are to get better.
- *Georg Christopher Lichtenberg*

No great improvements in the lot of mankind are possible until a great change
takes place in the fundamental constitution of their modes of thought.
- *John Stuart Mill*

Change is always **powerful**. Let your hook be always cast.
In the pool where you least expect it, will be a fish.
- Ovid

**Without change there is no innovation, creativity, or incentive for improvement.
Those who initiate change will have a better opportunity to manage
the change that is inevitable.**
- William Pollard

Progress is impossible without change;
and those who cannot change their minds cannot change anything.
- George Bernard Shaw

If we don't change, we don't grow. If we don't grow, we are not really living.
Growth demands a temporary surrender of security.
- Gail Sheehy

Change is the process by which the **future** invades our lives.
- Alvin Toffler

Many years ago,
when I was just about as complete a failure as
one can become,
I began to spend a good deal of time in
libraries, looking for some answers.
I found all the answers I needed in that golden
vein of ore that every library has.

- Og Mandino

Explore the World of Books

*A*s a professional speaker and humorist, Charlie "Tremendous" Jones traveled the world for more than forty years, delighting and challenging his audiences with his message that "Life Is Tremendous," and receiving just about every honor conferred in the speaking profession. A member of the Speakers' Hall of Fame, he was named one of the top fifty speakers of the twentieth century.

One of his great passions was instilling in his audiences the importance of reading, and he was famous for this statement: "You are the same today as you'll be in five years except for two things – the people you meet and the books you read." Many years ago, his company, Executive Books, published a four-volume series titled *The Books You Read*, containing hundreds of one-page summaries of books recommended by many of the famous and not-so-famous people whose lives have been impacted by a book.

Over the years, Charlie gave away hundreds of thousands of books. "I learned a long time ago," he said, "that I was wasting money by giving out business cards, which most people just throw away. So I started giving out books, with my name and phone number written inside. I can't tell you how many people have said to me that I'm the first person who has ever given them a book."

In a letter to a grandson, Charlie once offered these wise words: "Many people who you'll come to love will be met in books. Read biographies, autobiographies and history. Biographies will help you see there is nothing that can happen to you that wasn't experienced by many who used their failures, disappointments and tragedies as stepping stones for a more tremendous life."

Reading, indeed, is an important stepping-stone on the road to a more tremendous and successful life.

**A stone is not carved by a drop's falling twice, but by many times;
so too does a human not become wise by reading two, but by many books.**
- Giordano Bruno

What we **become** depends on what we read after all the professors
have finished with us. The greatest university of all is the collection of books.
- Thomas Carlyle

The way a book is read – which is to say, the **qualities** a reader brings to a
book – can have as much to do with its worth as anything the author puts in it.
Anyone who can read can learn to read deeply and thus live more fully.
- Norman Cousins

The reading of all good books is indeed like a conversation with the **noblest**
men of past centuries who were the authors of them, nay a carefully studied
conversation, in which they reveal to us none but the best of their thoughts.
- René Descartes

There is more **treasure** in books than in all the pirates' loot on Treasure Island…
and best of all, you can enjoy these riches **every day** of your life.
- Walt Disney

Books are the **quietest** and most **constant** of friends; they are the most accessible and wisest of counselors, and the most patient of **teachers**.
- *Charles W. Eliot*

Many times the reading of a book has made the **future** of a man.
- *Ralph Waldo Emerson*

The greatest gift is a **passion** for reading. It is cheap, it consoles, it distracts, it excites, it gives you knowledge of the world and experience of a wide kind. It is a moral **illumination**.
- *Elizabeth Hardwick*

Life-transforming **ideas** have always come to me through books.
- *Bell Hooks*

Every man who knows how to read has it in his power to magnify, to multiply the ways in which he exists, to make his life full, significant and interesting.
- *Aldous Huxley*

Don't read to be big, read to be down to earth. Don't read to be smart, read to be wise. Don't read to memorize, read to realize. Don't read to just learn, read to sometimes unlearn. Don't read a lot, read just enough to keep yourself **curious** and hungry, to learn more, to keep getting younger as you grow older.

- Charlie "Tremendous" Jones

If the book we are reading does not wake us, as with a fist hammering on our skull, why then do we read it? . . .
A book must be like an ice-axe to break the frozen sea within us.

- Franz Kafka

When you read the **best** books,
you will have as the guests of your mind the best thoughts of the best men.

- Grenville Kleiser

I love to **lose myself** in other men's minds. When I am not walking,
I am reading; I cannot sit and think. Books think for me.

- Charles Lamb

It is often said that one has but one life to live, but that is nonsense. For one who reads, there is **no limit** to the number of lives that may be lived, for fiction and biography and history offer an inexhaustible number of lives in many parts of the world, in all periods of time.

- Louis L'Amour

Language is the soul of intellect, and reading is the essential process by which that intellect is cultivated beyond the commonplace experiences of everyday life.
- Charles Scribner, Jr.

How many a man has dated a **new era** in his life from the reading of a book.
- Henry David Thoreau

Read an hour every day in your chosen field. This works out to about one book per week, 50 books per year, and will **guarantee** your **success**.
- Brian Tracy

Books are companions, teachers, magicians, bankers of the treasures of the mind. Books are **humanity in print**.
- Barbara Tuchman

The books I have read were composed by generations of fathers and sons, mothers and daughters, teachers and disciples.
I am the sum total of their experiences, and so are you.
- Elie Wiesel

Every man has a train of thought on which he travels when he is alone. The dignity and nobility of his life, as well as his happiness, depend upon the direction in which that train is going, the baggage it carries and the scenery through which it travels.

- Joseph Fort Newton

Your Thoughts Will Shape Your Destiny

*I*n Chapter 9, we introduced famed speaker Charlie "Tremendous" Jones, and the emphasis he placed on reading as a key tool for all who embark on the journey to success. But there was another tool he saw as just as important to take along on that journey.

In his presentations, he invariably instructed his audiences to not take any notes on what he was about to say. "Don't take notes on what a speaker says," he advised them. "Take notes on the thoughts you get from what you hear. You must learn to listen less and think more. The more you think, the more you realize that it doesn't do you any good to be smart. It's better to be plain and simple and real."

To illustrate his point, Charlie, with tongue firmly in cheek and a broad smile on his face, would tell of greeting his pastor after church on a Sunday morning and saying, "That was a great message this morning, pastor. You interrupted my train of thought five or six times."

Each of us is the engineer and the conductor on our own train of thought, fully responsible for keeping it pointed and moving in the right direction on the journey toward success.

Every great **achievement** in this world was first carefully thought out... **Think** – but to a purpose. Think constructively... Think to rise and improve your place in life. There can be no advancement or **success** without serious thought.
- *George Matthew Adams*

Thoughts mean life, since those who do not think do not live in any high or real sense.
- *Amos Bronson Alcott*

You are today where your thoughts have **brought** you; you will be tomorrow where your thoughts **take** you.
- *James Lane Allen*

Such as are your habitual thoughts, such also will be the **character** of your mind; for the soul is dyed by the thoughts. Dye it then with a continuous series of such thoughts as these: for instance, that where a man can live, there he can also **live well**.
- *Marcus Aurelius*

Don't keep forever on the public road. **Leave** the beaten path occasionally and dive into the woods. You will be certain to find something that you have never seen before. One **discovery** will lead to another, and before you know it you will have something worth thinking about to occupy your mind. All really big discoveries are the results of **thoughts**.
- *Alexander Graham Bell*

Our thought is the **key** which unlocks the doors of the world.
- Samuel McC. Crothers

I have within my **heart** an inmate, even my thought,
which shapes for me my **destiny**.
- Ella E. Dodson

We must **dare** to think 'unthinkable' thoughts. We must learn to **explore** all the options and possibilities that confront us in a complex and rapidly changing world. We must learn to welcome and not to fear the voices of dissent. We must dare to think about 'unthinkable things' because when things become unthinkable, thinking stops and **action** becomes mindless.
- J. William Fulbright

If you don't think you can do it, who will?
You control the most important tool in success, your mind.
- Jeffrey Gitomer

You have **absolute control** over but one thing, and that is your thoughts. This is the most significant and inspiring of all facts known to man!
It reflects man's **divine nature**.
- Napoleon Hill

Once you **wake up** thought in a man, you can never put it to sleep again.
- Zora Neale Hurston

Project the thought of success and half the battle is won.
- Sybil Leek

To think is to **meander** from highway to byway, and from byway to alleyway, till we come to a dead end. Stopped dead in our alley, we think what a feat it would be to get out. That is when we look for the gate to the **meadows** beyond.
- Antonio Machado

What we think about is constantly weaving itself into the **fabric** of our career, becoming a part of ourselves, increasing the power of our mental magnet to attract those things which we most ardently desire.
- Orison Swett Marden

People become really quite **remarkable** when they start thinking that they can do things. When they believe in themselves, they have the first **secret** of success.
- Norman Vincent Peale

If you think about disaster, you will get it. Brood about death and you hasten your demise. Think **positively** and masterfully, with confidence and faith, and life becomes more secure, more fraught with action, richer in **achievement** and experience.
- Eddie Rickenbacker

The **task** is not so much to see what no one yet has seen,
but to think what nobody yet has thought about that which everybody sees.
- Arthur Schopenhauer

Thought is the sculptor who can create the person you want to be.
- Henry David Thoreau

Thinking is the place where **intelligent** actions begin. We pause long enough to look more carefully at a situation, to see more of its **character**, to think about why it's happening, to notice how it's affecting us and others.
- Margaret J. Wheatley

Are you willing to think? Consider carefully, for the answer to that question will largely determine your **success** or failure in life. If you would develop your judgment, use it. Exercise your power of judgment as often as you can, for the **first rule** of good judgment is practice. The functions of your mind, no less than the muscles of your body, receive their strength through repeated use.
- John M. Wilson

Success at almost anything doesn't just happen. In almost every area of your life, the more you prepare, the better the result will be.

- Joel H. Weldon

Be Prepared

*J*oel Weldon has been one of America's most successful and respected professional speakers for more than three decades. In 1989, he was honored as the recipient of the Golden Gavel, the most prestigious award conferred by Toastmasters International. Other winners have included such illustrious names as Walter Cronkite, Earl Nightingale, Art Linkletter, Ken Blanchard and Stephen Covey.

Weldon has also been inducted into the National Speakers Hall of Fame and, in 2006, was named a "Legend of the Speaking Profession." He's known worldwide for his unique trademark, a heavy 8-ounce can which sits on the desks of thousands of his clients and customers, with a label that reads: "Success Comes In CANS, Not In Cannots!"

Asked the secret of his success, he cites several factors, including preparation. Although he has given more than 2,800 presentations, he says: "As a professional speaker for more than 35 years, I still invest 50 hours to prepare for each of my custom keynote speeches and seminars. Why? Because to be excellent, I know each idea presented must relate specifically to the audience."

He adds, "Excellence is the result of effort and preparation. How much time are you willing to invest in order to be amazing at what you do – so people can only describe your results as excellent? It's one of the keys to your success."

Before anything else, preparation is the key to success.
- Alexander Graham Bell

It's not the will to **win** that matters—everyone has that.
It's the will to **prepare** to win that matters.
- Paul "Bear" Bryant

There is no short cut to **achievement**.
Life requires thorough preparation – veneer isn't worth anything.
- George Washington Carver

Forewarned, forearmed; to be prepared is **half** the victory.
Wisdom comes of such a recognition.
- Miguel de Cervantes

Be ready when opportunity comes…
Luck is the time when **preparation** and **opportunity** meet.
- Roy D. Chapin Jr.

In all things, success depends upon previous **preparation**, and without such preparation there is sure to be failure.
- Confucius

I believe success is preparation, because **opportunity** is going to knock on your door sooner or later but are you prepared to answer?
- Omar Epps

By failing to prepare you are preparing to fail.
- Benjamin Franklin

None of us suddenly becomes something overnight. The **preparations** have been in the making for a **lifetime**.
- Gail Kathleen Godwin

We are all, it seems, saving ourselves for the Senior Prom. But many of us forget that somewhere along the way we must **learn to dance**.
- Alan Harrington

No man ever reached to **excellence** in any one art or profession without having passed through the slow and painful process of study and preparation.
- Horace

There is no road too long to the man who advances **deliberately** and without undue haste; there are no **honors** too distant to the man who prepares himself for them with patience.
- Jean de La Bruyère

I fear not the man who has practiced 10,000 kicks once, but I fear the man who has practiced one kick 10,000 times.
- Bruce Lee

I will **prepare** and some day my chance will come.
- Abraham Lincoln

You better live your **best** and act your best and think your best today, for today is the sure **preparation** for tomorrow and all the other tomorrows that follow.
- Harriet Martineau

Live neither in the past nor in the future, but let each day's work absorb all your **interest**, **energy** and **enthusiasm**. The best preparation for tomorrow is to do today's work superbly well.
- *Sir William Osler*

The will to win is **important**, but the will to prepare is **vital**.
- *Joe Paterno*

There are no secrets to success.
It is the result of preparation, hard work, learning from failure.
- *Colin C. Powell*

Spectacular **achievement** is always preceded by unspectacular **preparation.**
- *Robert H. Schuller*

Excellence is never cheap. It is costly.
Constant care, serious preparation and continual application are required.
Excellence involves desire plus discipline plus determination.
- *George Sweeting*

You will never stub your toe standing still.
The faster you go, the more chance there is of
stubbing your toe, but the more chance
you have of getting somewhere.

- Charles F. Kettering

Go Ahead! Get Started!

In 1840, American educator Thomas H. Palmer published a book, titled *Teacher's Manual*, which included a short poem. While few of us today would recognize Palmer's name, we're probably all familiar with this poem:

'Tis a lesson you should heed,
Try, try again.
If at first you don't succeed,
Try, try again.

That could have been the theme song of Charles F. Kettering. In fact, Kettering once said: "It doesn't matter if you try and try and try again, and fail. It does matter if you try and fail, and fail to try again."

Born in 1876, he earned an engineering degree and joined National Cash Register Company, where he developed the first electrically operated cash register. He then turned his attention to the fledgling automotive industry, co-founding Dayton Engineering Laboratories Corporation, which later became Delco, and was acquired by General Motors.

It was Kettering who invented the electric self-starter for automobiles. In 1910, he joined GM, remaining there until 1947. His genius, however, was by no means limited to automobiles. He invented such breakthrough technologies in health care as a treatment for venereal disease, an incubator for premature infants, and artificial fever therapy.

Other inventions included: the electrically operated gate and a lightweight diesel engine for the railroads; the first synthetic aviation fuel; shock absorbers, safety glass and automatic transmissions for automobiles; and Freon for refrigerators and air conditioners. In his lifetime, he held more than 300 patents.

Kettering was a man of action, who never allowed fear of failure to slow him down. He called failures "finger posts on the road to achievement," adding that "one fails forward to success." His philosophy was to "keep on going," and not to worry about failing, "because every failure is one more step leading up to the cathedral of success."

Whatever you do, do it with all your **might**. Work at it, early and late, in season and out of season, not leaving a stone unturned, and never deferring for a single hour that which can be done just as well as now.
- Phineas T. Barnum

Inspirations never go in for long engagements;
they demand immediate marriage to **action**.
- Brendan Francis Behan

You don't have to **be great** to get started,
but you have to get started to be great.
- Les Brown

The way to get started is to quit talking and begin doing.
- Walt Disney

Take action. Procrastination is the death blow to self-motivation.
"I'll do it later... after I get organized" is the language of the unsuccessful and
the frustrated. Successful, highly **motivated** men and women don't put it off.
- Ted W. Engstrom

Why wait? Life is not a dress rehearsal.
Quit practicing what you are going to do, and **just do it**.
- Marilyn Grey

The vision must be followed by the **venture**. It is not enough to stare up the steps
– we must step up the stairs.
- Vance Havner

The person who is waiting for something to turn up
might start with their shirt sleeves.
- Garth Henrichs

Somewhere in your make-up there lies sleeping the seed of **achievement**
which, if aroused and put into action, would carry you to heights
such as you may never have hoped to **attain**.
- Napoleon Hill

Parties who want **milk** should not seat themselves on a stool
in the middle of a field in hope that the **COW** will back up to them.
- Elbert Hubbard

So what do we do? Anything. Something. So long as we just don't sit there. If we screw it up, start over. **Try something else**. If we wait until we've satisfied all the uncertainties, it may be too late.
- Lee Iacocca

Take time to **deliberate**;
but when the time for action arrives, stop thinking and go in.
- Andrew Jackson

Things may come to those who wait, but only the things left by those who hustle.
- Abraham Lincoln

Begin somewhere; you cannot build a reputation on what you intend to do.
- James Russell Lowell

Even if it doesn't work,
there is something **healthy** and **invigorating** about direct action.
- Henry Miller

Action is a great restorer and builder of confidence.
Inaction is not only the result, but the cause, of fear. Perhaps the action you take
will be **successful**; perhaps different action or adjustments will have to follow.
But any action is better than no action at all.
- *Norman Vincent Peale*

Indecision is fatal. It is better to make a wrong decision than build up
a habit of indecision. If you're wallowing in indecision,
you certainly can't act—and **action** is the basis of **success**.
- *Marie Beynon Ray*

Get action. Do things; be sane, don't fritter away your time; create, act,
take a place wherever you are and **be somebody**; get action.
- *Theodore Roosevelt*

You're going to have to find out where you want to go. And then you've
got to start going there. But **immediately**. You can't afford to lose a minute.
- *J.D. Salinger*

We know what a person thinks, not when he tells us what he thinks,
but by his actions.
- *Isaac Bashevis Singer*

A strong will, a settled purpose,
an invincible determination,
can accomplish almost anything;
and in this lies the distinction
between great men and little men.

- Thomas Fuller

Never Give Up!

*T*he year was 1983. In Australia, the long-distance foot race from Sydney to Melbourne was about to begin, covering 875 kilometers – more than 500 miles! About 150 world-class athletes had entered, for what was planned as a six-day event. So race officials were startled when a 61-year-old man approached and handed them his entry form.

His name was Cliff Young, and his "racing attire" included overalls and galoshes over his work boots.

At first, they refused to let him enter. So he explained that he'd grown up on a 2,000-acre farm, with thousands of sheep. His family could afford neither horses nor tractors so, when the storms came, his job was to round up the sheep. Sometimes, he said, it would take two or three days of running.

Finally, they let Cliff enter, and the race began. The others quickly left him way behind, shuffling along in his galoshes. But he didn't know the plan included stopping each night to rest, so he kept going.

By the fifth day, he had caught them all, won the race, and became a national hero. He continued to compete in long-distance races until well up in his seventies. He was an inspiration to millions and a great encourager of younger runners.

In his honor and memory, in 2004, the year after his death at age 81, the organizers of the race where he first gained fame permanently changed its name to the Cliff Young Australian Six Day Race.

What was the key to Cliff Young's success? It goes by various names: determination, perseverance, persistence, tenacity. It means keeping one's eye fixed steadfastly on a goal, and not stopping, no matter the difficulties or the obstacles, until that goal is achieved.

Desire is the key to **motivation**, but it's determination and commitment to an unrelenting pursuit of your goal – a commitment to **excellence** – that will enable you to attain the success you seek.
- Mario Andretti

Success is reached by being active, awake, ahead of the crowd, by aiming high, pushing ahead, honestly, diligently, patiently; by climbing, digging, saving; by forgetting the past, using the present, trusting in the future; by honoring God, having a purpose, fainting not, determining to win, and striving to the end.
- Russell Conwell

Perseverance is not a long race; it is many short races one after another.
- Walter Elliott

A determination to succeed is the only way to **succeed** that I know anything about.
- William Feather

Do your work with your whole **heart**, and you will succeed – there's so little competition.
- Elbert Hubbard

We can do anything we want to if we stick to it long enough.
- Helen Keller

The difference between the impossible and the possible
lies in a person's **determination**.
- Tommy Lasorda

Perseverance is a great element of success. If you only knock long enough
and loud enough at the gate, you are sure to wake somebody.
- Henry Wadsworth Longfellow

So long as there is breath in me, that long will I **persist**. For now I know one of
the greatest principles of success: if I persist long enough I will win.
- Og Mandino

If you would **succeed** in life, it is of first importance that your individuality, your
independence, your determination be trained that you not be lost in the crowd.
- Orison Swett Marden

Bear in mind, if you are going to amount to anything, that your success does not depend upon the **brilliancy** and the impetuosity with which you take hold, but upon the everlasting and sanctified bull-doggedness with which you hang on after you have taken hold.
- Dr. A.B. Meldrum

Have the dogged determination to follow through to achieve your goal, regardless of circumstances or whatever other people say, think, or do.
- Paul Meyer

It is not enough to begin; **continuance** is necessary... Success depends upon staying power. The reason for failure in most cases is lack of perseverance.
- J.R. Miller

A **steadfast** soul, holding steadily to a dream ideal, plus a sturdy will determined to succeed in any venture, can make any dream come true.
- B.N. Mills

To tend, unfailingly, unflinchingly, towards a goal, is the **secret** of success.
- Anna Pavlova

Singleness of purpose is one of the chief **essentials** for success in life,
no matter what may be one's aim.
- John D. Rockefeller

You just can't beat the person who never gives up.
- Babe Ruth

Whatever the struggle, **continue** the climb.
It may be only one step to the summit.
- Diane Westlake

There is no chance, no destiny, no fate that can circumvent or hinder
or control the firm resolve of a **determined soul**.
- Ella Wheeler Wilcox

I know the price of **success**: dedication, hard work and
an unremitting devotion to the things you want to see happen.
- Frank Lloyd Wright

We keep moving forward, opening new doors, and doing new things, because we're curious and curiosity keeps leading us down new paths.

- Walt Disney

Discover New Paths

Richard P. Feynman, who died in 1970, at age 69, was an American physicist and one of the best-known scientists in the world, credited with many breakthrough discoveries in his chosen field. Early in his career, he was part of the team which developed the atom bomb and, years later, he served on the panel appointed to investigate the Space Shuttle Challenger disaster. In 1965, he was one of three recipients of the Nobel Prize in Physics, and he served for many years as a professor at the prestigious California Institute of Technology.

Feynman also had a less serious side, often seen as a "free spirit" and something of an eccentric. He enjoyed writing and painting, playing bongo drums, juggling, picking locks and practical jokes. While at Los Alamos, where the atom bomb was developed, he spent his spare time picking the locks of cabinets which contained highly classified secrets, and leaving mysterious notes for his colleagues, implying that foreign agents had gained access.

What drove Feynman, both in his serious and frivolous pursuits, was an insatiably curious mind, as illustrated by the titles of two of his books. The first: *Surely You're Joking, Mr. Feynman*, was subtitled *Adventures of a Curious Character*. It was followed by: *What Do You Care What Other People Think?*, subtitled *Further Adventures of a Curious Character*.

Feynman credited his father for encouraging him, from childhood, to challenge accepted thinking. "I was born not knowing," he once said, "and have had only a little time to change that here and there."

He may have had, in his words, "only a little time," but he used it well. It was Richard Feynman's curiosity that, in Walt Disney's words, kept leading him "down new paths," and brought him such great success.

Research is formalized **curiosity**. It is poking and prying with a purpose.
- Zora Neale Hurston

Be curious always! For knowledge will not acquire you; you must acquire it.
- Sudie Back

You can teach a student a lesson for a day; but if you can teach him to learn by creating curiosity, he will continue the **learning** process as long as he lives.
- Clay P. Bedford

A sense of curiosity is nature's **original** school of education.
- Smiley Blanton

The first and simplest **emotion** which we discover in the human mind is **curiosity**.
- Edmund Burke

Curiosity about **life** in all of its aspects,
I think, is still the secret of great **creative** people.
- Leo Burnett

Curiosity is free-wheeling **intelligence**… It endows the people who have it
with a generosity in argument and a serenity in their own mode of life which
spring from the **cheerful** willingness to let life take the forms it will.
- Alistair Cooke

What is a scientist after all? It is a **curious man** looking through a keyhole,
the keyhole of nature, trying to know what is going on.
- Jacques Cousteau

Curiosity has its own reason for existing. One cannot help but be in **awe** when
he contemplates the mysteries of eternity, of life, of the marvelous
structure of **reality**. It is enough if one tries merely to comprehend a little
of this mystery every day. Never lose a holy curiosity.
- Albert Einstein

Curiosity is one of the permanent and certain characteristics of a vigorous intellect.
- Samuel Johnson

Curiosity is, in **great** and **generous** minds, the first passion and the last.
- Samuel Johnson

There are two sorts of curiosity – the momentary and the permanent.
The **momentary** is concerned with the odd appearance on the surface of
things. The **permanent** is attracted by the amazing and consecutive life that
flows on beneath the surface of things.
- Robert S. Lynd

A curious person who asks questions may be a fool for five minutes;
he who never asks questions remains a fool forever.
- Vern McLellan

The cure for boredom is **curiosity**. There is no cure for curiosity.
- Ellen Parr

One of the secrets of life is to keep our intellectual **curiosity** acute.
- William Lyon Phelps

Curiosity is an instinct of infinite scope: on the one hand it leads to listening behind closed doors; on the other, it leads to the **discovery** of America.
- Jose Maria Queiros

Life was meant to be **lived**, and curiosity must be kept alive.
One must never, for whatever reason, turn his back on life.
- Eleanor Roosevelt

Curiosity will conquer fear even more than **bravery** will; indeed it has led many people into dangers which mere physical courage would shudder away from, for hunger and love and curiosity are the great impelling forces of life.
- James Stephens

Curiosity is the wick in the candle of learning.
- William Arthur Ward

Life can be one dreary day after another or a Baghdad of fascinating things to keep learning. Get more out of every phase of your life – stay incurably curious.
- L. Perry Wilbur

Why is asking questions such an important part of
life? We simply cannot make clear distinctions
without the use of questions! No distinctions!
No decisions! No actions! No wonder questions
are such a powerful force. Without questions,
we would not could not take any action!

- Bobb Biehl

Keep Asking Questions

*B*obb Biehl has been asking questions for more than 30 years. In 1976, after a successful career with a leading nonprofit organization, he founded Masterplanning Group International. An executive mentor, he has consulted with more than 2,500 executives in businesses, churches, nonprofit groups and government agencies.

Biehl is a firm believer in the power of questions as an important component of success. "No problem in the world," he says, "has ever been solved without a question or series of questions being asked first. Learning to ask is a prerequisite to learning to think clearly. If you are not able to ask questions, you will ultimately make cloudy distinctions, reach uncertain decisions, and take wrong actions."

In *The Question Book*, published in 1993, Biehl called on ninety experts to each submit a series of twenty questions covering virtually every aspect of life, including business, education, health, marriage and family, politics, religion and finances. His firm has also published *Asking to Win*, containing more than one hundred profound questions to help readers make wise decisions for a lifetime.

One man told us this story: "My senior level position had been unexpectedly eliminated, and I didn't know what to do next. I knew Bobb slightly, and visited with him one afternoon. He began asking me a few insightful questions about things I'd never even considered. As a result of one particular question, I set off on an entirely new career path which, nearly three decades later, continues to bring me satisfaction and success."

That question Bobb Biehl asked, which started our friend along the road to success, echoed a statement once made by Hamilton Wright Mabie, a well-known American essayist and lecturer of a century ago: "The question for each man to settle is not what he would do if he had means, time, influence and educational advantages, but what he will do with the things he has."

"How do you know so much about **everything**?" was asked of a very wise and intelligent man; and the answer was "By never being afraid or ashamed to ask questions as to anything of which I was ignorant."
- *John Abbott*

The first key to **wisdom** is assidious and frequent questioning....
For by doubting we come to inquiry, and by inquiry we arrive at **truth**.
- *Peter Abelard*

Who questions much, shall **learn** much, and retain much.
- *Francis Bacon*

The art and science of asking questions is the source of all knowledge.
- *Thomas Berger*

My greatest **strength** as a consultant is to be ignorant and ask a few questions.
- *Peter F. Drucker*

The **important** thing is not to stop questioning.
- Albert Einstein

It is a poor and disgraceful thing not to be able to reply, with some degree of certainty, to the simple **questions**, "What will you be? What will you do?"
- John Foster

Don't be afraid to ask dumb questions.
They're more easily handled than dumb mistakes.
- William Wister Haines

If you don't ask the right questions, you don't get the right answers.
A question asked in the right way often points to its own **answer**.
Asking questions is the ABC of diagnosis. Only the inquiring mind solves problems.
- Edward Hodnett

To be on a quest is nothing more or less than to become an **asker** of questions.
- Sam Keen

Questions are the creative acts of **intelligence**.
- Frank Kingdon

The wise man doesn't give the right **answers**, he poses the right **questions**.
- Claude Levi-Strauss

Nothing shapes our **journey** through life so much as the questions we ask.
- Gregg Levoy

You can tell whether a man is clever by his answers.
You can tell whether a man is wise by his questions.
- Naguib Manfouz

Successful people ask **better** questions, and as a result,
they get better answers.
- Tony Robbins

It's a healthy **idea** to hang a question mark on the things
you have long taken for granted.
- Bertrand Russell

The key to wisdom is knowing all the right questions.
- John A. Simone Jr.

There are no foolish questions,
and no man becomes a fool until he has **stopped** asking questions.
- Charles P. Steinmetz

Success is **achieved** by those who try and those who ask.
- W. Clement Stone

Ask yourself the **easy** questions and you will have a hard life.
Ask yourself the **hard** questions and you will have an easy life.
- Peter Thompson

Nobody ever got into any trouble listening.
That's about the safest thing that one can do in life.
If you listen to people and you pay attention to them,
then you're bound to learn.

- James O'Toole

Listen and Learn

*T*he late Steve Allen, who launched The Tonight Show in 1954, enjoyed involving his audiences in his shows. Often, he'd leave the stage and whisper a brief statement to someone sitting in an aisle seat, and ask that person to whisper it to the next person, with the process continuing across the row. The person in the last seat was asked to repeat the statement aloud.

At the same time, the original statement was flashed on the screen. Invariably, there was great disparity, leading to much laughter. But the sobering point it made, again and again, is that we're a nation of non-listeners.

In the 1980s, a California-based consultant named Ben Joyce had had enough. "Listening," he said, "is a skill that has a dreadfully limited number of truly effective practitioners. We're not taught to listen in school, at home, or at work. On the contrary, we learn the communications process from authority figures whose specialty seems to be talking."

Joyce decided to do something, designing a device he called "The Listening Stick." The small wooden stick was imprinted on one side with the words: "Please, will you listen to me?" On the reverse side were the words: "Thank you." Accompanying it was a detailed instruction brochure, called "An Owner's Manual," and a business-card size "Quick Use Guide."

The plan was to politely hand the stick to so-called "listeners," who had "the attention span of a flashbulb," or "listened with a stop watch," or quickly took over the speaking role.

Sadly, Joyce's noble experiment had limited success, and we continue to be mostly non-listeners, despite the many advantages accrued to those who have developed strong listening skills. As the late Bernard M. Baruch, an American financier and presidential advisor, noted: "Most of the successful people I've known are those who do more listening than talking."

It's just as important to listen to someone with your eyes as it is with your ears.
- *Martin Buxbaum*

To live without **listening** is not to live at all;
it is simply to drift in my own backwater.
- *Joan Chittister*

Most people do not listen with the intent to **understand**, rather they listen with
the intent to reply. They are busy filtering everything through their own
perspectives rather than trying to understand another's frame of reference.
- *Stephen R. Covey*

The effects of really good listening can be **dramatic**.
These effects include the satisfied customer who will come back,
the **contented** employee who will stay with the company,
the manager who has the **trust** of his staff,
and the salesman who tops his quota.
- *John L. DiGaetani*

You must possess, at the same time, the habit of **communicating** and
the habit of listening. The union is rather rare, but irresistible.
- *Benjamin Disraeli*

Instead of talking in the **hope** that people will listen,
try listening to people in the hope that they will talk.
- Dr. Mardy Grothe

Listen is such a little, ordinary word. Yet we all know the pain of not being
listened to, of not being **heard**... In a way, not to be heard is not to exist.
- Margaret Guenther

The more faithfully you listen to the voice within you, the better you will hear
what is sounding outside. And only he who listens can speak.
- Dag Hammarskjöld

I like to listen. I have **learned** a great deal from listening carefully.
Most people never listen.
- Ernest Hemingway

It is the province of **knowledge** to speak.
And it is the privilege of **wisdom** to listen.
- Oliver Wendell Holmes, Jr.

If you listen, you can **learn**;
if you talk, you can merely repeat that which you **believe** to be true.
- Ben Joyce

Be different – if you don't have the facts and knowledge required, simply listen. When word gets out that you can listen when others tend to talk, you will be treated as a sage.
- Edward Koch

Then I want to sit and **listen** and have someone talk,
tell me things... Not to say anything – to listen and listen and **be taught**.
- Anne Morrow Lindbergh

Listening is an active pursuit that requires skill and practice.
- Stacey Lucas

Formula for handling people:
1) Listen to the other person's **story**;
2) Listen to the other person's **full story**;
3) Listen to the other person's **full story first**.
- General George C. Marshall

Listening well is as powerful a means
of **communication** and influence as to talk well.
- Supreme Court Justice John Marshall

One friend, one person who is **truly** understanding,
who takes the trouble to **listen** to us as we consider our problem,
can **change** our whole outlook on the world.
- Elton Mayo

Listening is a magnetic and strange thing, **a creative force**...
When we are listened to, it creates us, makes us unfold and expand.
- Karl Menninger

**A good listener is not only popular everywhere,
but after a while he knows something.**
- Wilson Mizner

You cannot truly **listen** to anyone and do **anything** else at the same time.
- M. Scott Peck

Enthusiasm is one of the most powerful engines of success. When you do a thing, do it with all your might. Put your whole soul into it. Stamp it with your own personality. Be active, be energetic, be enthusiastic and faithful, and you will accomplish your objective. Nothing great was ever achieved without enthusiasm.

- Ralph Waldo Emerson

Be Enthusiastic - Always!

Gordon Parks was a remarkable man, who accomplished much in his lifetime, despite a start that seemed bleak – at best. He was born in 1912, the youngest of 15 children in a poverty-stricken Kansas family. After his mother's death when he was 15, he dropped out of school and left home, supporting himself as a busboy, waiter, semipro basketball player, self-taught piano player and big band singer.

But, before her death, his mother had planted a seed in Gordon that would later bear fruit. "She would not allow me to complain," he said, "about not accomplishing something because I was black. Her attitude was: 'If a white boy can do it, then you can do it, too – and do it better.'"

While in his twenties, he became interested in photography, and purchased a pawnshop camera for $12.50. That marked the start of a distinguished career, including 20 years as a photographer for *Life* magazine.

But Parks' interests extended well beyond photography. He wrote poetry and several books, composed a piano concerto and the music for a ballet. He went on to become the first African-American to direct a Hollywood movie, and his film, Shaft, received an Academy Award. In 1988, President Ronald Reagan presented him with the National Medal of Arts in honor of his life of achievements.

Gordon Parks died in 2006 at the age of 93 – a one-time high school dropout who had received more than 40 honorary degrees. What was the secret of his remarkable success? It can be described in a single word – enthusiasm. "Enthusiasm," he wrote, "is the electricity of life. How do you get it? You act enthusiastic until you make it a habit. Enthusiasm is natural; it is being alive, taking the initiative, seeing the importance of what you do, giving it dignity and making what you do important to yourself and to others."

Enthusiasm is the inspiration of **everything great**.
Without it no man is to be feared, and with it none despised.
- Christian N. Bovée

Nothing is so contagious as enthusiasm.
- Edward Bulwer-Lytton

Every man is **enthusiastic** at times.
One man has enthusiasm for thirty minutes – another man has it for thirty days,
but it is the man who has it for thirty years who makes a **success** in life.
- Edward B. Butler

Enthusiasm, backed up by horse sense and persistence,
is the **quality** that most frequently makes for success.
- Dale Carnegie

Enthusiasm is the **greatest asset** in the world.
It beats money and power and influence.
It is no more or less than faith in action.
- Henry Chester

Get excited and enthusiastic about you own **dream**.
This excitement is like a forest fire –
you can **smell** it, **taste** it, and **see** it from a mile away.
- Stephen Covey

Every production of **genius** must be the production of enthusiasm.
- Benjamin Disraeli

Enthusiasm is at the bottom of all progress.
With it there is **accomplishment**.
Without it there are only alibis.
- Henry Ford

A mother should give her children a **superabundance** of enthusiasm,
that after they have lost all they are sure to lose on mixing with the world,
enough may still remain to prompt and support them through **great actions**.
- Julius C. Hare

Enthusiasm finds the opportunities, and energy makes the most of them.
- Henry S. Haskins

Follow your enthusiasm. It's something I've always believed in. Find those parts of your life you enjoy the most. Do what you enjoy doing.

- Jim Henson

Study the unusually **successful** people you know,
and you will find them imbued with enthusiasm for their work which is **contagious**.
Not only are they themselves **excited** about what they are doing,
but they also get you excited.

- Paul W. Ivey

We act as though comfort and luxury were the chief **requirements** of life,
when all that we need to make us really happy is something to be enthusiastic about.

- Charles Kingsley

Live neither in the past nor in the future,
but let each day's work absorb all your **interest**, **energy** and **enthusiasm**.

- Sir William Osler

There is real **magic** in enthusiasm.
It spells the difference between mediocrity and **accomplishment**.

- Norman Vincent Peale

A man will **succeed** at anything about which he is really enthusiastic.
- Charles M. Schwab

Apathy can be overcome by **enthusiasm**,
and enthusiasm can be aroused by two things:
first, an **idea** which takes the imagination by storm;
and second, a definite, intelligible **plan** for carrying that idea into action.
- Arnold Toynbee

You don't ever want to sleep when you're enthusiastic. If you can't wait to get up until
tomorrow to get back to work on something, then you won't sleep much anyway.
- Jim Trebig

Where does enthusiasm come from?
Is it the end result of an **achievement** or is it the reason for that achievement—
that success? It's **both**! But without enthusiasm, there's little hope of success.
- Joel H. Weldon

Catch on fire with **enthusiasm** and people will come for miles to watch you burn.
- John Wesley

I have only just a minute,
Only sixty seconds in it.
Forced upon me, can't refuse it.
Didn't seek it, didn't choose it.
But it's up to me to use it,
I must suffer if I lose it,
Give account if I abuse it.
Just a tiny little minute,
But eternity is in it.

- Christine Warren

Make Every Minute Count

*T*ime! Over the course of history, it has been defined or described in more ways perhaps than there are hours in a month (700+), or minutes in a day (1440). Observations about time include the comical, the cynical and the serious.

Novelist Faith Baldwin called time "a dressmaker specializing in alterations," while author Lucille S. Harper described it as "a great healer but a poor beautician." Screenwriter and playwright Ben Hecht saw it as "a circus, always packing up and moving away." To business executive Franklin P. Jones: "Time is a versatile performer. It flies, marches on, heals all wounds, runs out, and will tell."

Others have taken a more serious view, calling time: "the life of the soul" (Longfellow); "the coin of your life" (Sandburg); "the only capital that any human being has" (Edison); and "the stuff life is made of" (Benjamin Franklin).

Making the best use of one's time is a key ingredient in the formula for success. The late Peter F. Drucker, often called "the father of modern management," was a leading exponent of the importance of time management, emphasizing it often in many of his 39 books and countless newspaper and journal articles.

"Time," Drucker wrote, "is always in short supply. There is no substitute for time. Everything requires time. It is the only truly universal condition. All work takes place in, and uses up time. Yet most people take for granted this unique, irreplaceable and necessary resource."

Drucker, until well up into his nineties, consulted with many Fortune 500 companies and some of the world's best known business leaders. His admonition to them is the same as it is for all who would achieve success today: "Time is the scarcest resource, and unless it is managed, nothing else can be managed."

Have regular hours for work and play; make each day both useful and pleasant, and prove that you understand the worth of time by employing it well. Then… life will become **a beautiful success**.
- Louisa May Alcott

Since **time** is the one immaterial object which we cannot influence – neither speed up nor slow down, add to nor diminish – it is an **imponderably valuable** gift.
- Maya Angelou

Be wise in the use of time. The question of life is not, How much time have we? The question is, What shall we do with it?
- Anna Robertson Brown

Don't say you don't have enough time. You have **exactly** the same number of hours per day that were given to Helen Keller, Pasteur, Michelangelo, Mother Teresa, Leonardo da Vinci, Thomas Jefferson and Albert Einstein.
- H. Jackson Brown

Much may be done in those little **shreds** and **patches** of time which every day produces and which most men throw away.
- Charles Caleb Colton

Those who **succeed** are those who have thoroughly learned the immense importance of **plan** in life, and the tragic brevity of time.
- W.J. Davison

Guard well your spare moments. They are like uncut diamonds. Discard them and their value will never be known. **Improve** them and they will become the brightest gems in a **useful** life.
- Ralph Waldo Emerson

A **wise** person does at once, what a fool does at last. Both do the same thing; only at different times.
- Baltasar Gracian

Time is everything. Anything you want, anything you accomplish pleasure, success, fortune is measured in time.
- Joyce C. Hall

Time is a fixed income and, as with any income, the real problem facing most of us is how to **live successfully** within our daily allotment.
- Margaret B. Johnstone

Determine never to be idle. No person will have occasion to complain of the want of time, who never loses any.
It is **wonderful** how much may be done, if we are always doing.
- Thomas Jefferson

It is **wise** to think about the past and learn from it. But it is unwise for us to be in the past... It is also wise for us to **think** about the future and plan for it.
But it is unwise for us to be in the future...
The present moment is the only **reality** we will ever experience.
- Spencer Johnson

Today is your day and mine, the only day we have, the day in which we play our part.
What our part may signify in the **great** whole we may not understand;
but we are here to play it, and now is the **time**.
- David Starr Jordan

In truth, people can generally make time for what they choose to do;
it is not really the time but the will that is lacking.
- Sir John Lubbock

We are not living in eternity. We have only this **moment**, sparkling like a star in our hand – and melting like a snowflake, Let us **use it** before it is too late.
- Marie Beynon Ray

Yesterday is a memory; tomorrow is an imagination; today is eternity.
Cut out two days of your life, yesterday with its mistakes,
tomorrow with its fears, and **live only today**.
- Virgil A. Reed

Now is the watchword of the wise.
- Charles H. Spurgeon

There is no sudden leap to **greatness**. Your success lies in **doing**, day by day.
- Max Steingart

You must live in the **present**, launch yourself on every wave,
find your eternity in **each moment**.
Fools stand on their island of opportunities and look toward another land.
- Henry David Thoreau

To get all there is out of living, we must employ our time **wisely**,
never being in too much of a hurry to **stop and sip** life,
but never losing our sense of the enormous **value of a minute**.
- Robert D. Updegraff

The common denominator
of success - the secret of
success of every man who
has ever been successful - lies
in the fact that he formed the
habit of doing things that
failures don't like to do.

- Albert E.N. Gray

Your Habits Form Your Future

*I*n 1940, the National Association of Life Underwriters held its annual meeting in Philadelphia. At one of the general sessions, the speaker was Albert E.N. Gray, an official of The Prudential Insurance Company of America, who, during a 30-year career with that company, had become known nationally as a writer and speaker on life insurance subjects.

As he rose to speak on that long-ago day, it probably didn't occur to Gray that his message would become a classic, applicable not only to the members of his profession but to all who would seek success in any endeavor.

"Several years ago," he began, "I was brought face to face with the very disturbing realization that I was trying to supervise and direct the efforts of a large number of men who were trying to achieve success, without knowing myself what the secret of success really was."

So Gray launched what he called a voyage of discovery to learn that secret. "It must not only apply," he said, "to every definition of success, but since it must apply to everyone to whom it was offered, it must also apply to everyone who had ever been successful. In short, I was looking for the common denominator of success."

After studying the lives of many successful individuals, Gray found that common denominator, as described in the words which introduce this chapter – forming the habit of doing things failures don't like to do.

"Every single qualification for success," he insisted, "is acquired through habit. Men form habits and habits form futures."

Nearly two centuries ago, American theologian Nathanael Emmons commented that "habit is either the best of servants or the worst of masters." Those who would become successful, then, will be wise to choose those servants who will help them reach their goals.

Excellence is an art won by **training** and **habituation**.
We do not act rightly because we have virtue or excellence,
but rather we have those because we have acted rightly.
We are what we repeatedly do.
Excellence, then, is not an act but **a habit**.
- Aristotle

Such as are your habitual thoughts, such also will be the **character** of your mind;
for the soul is dyed by the thoughts. Dye it then with a continuous series of such
thoughts as these: for instance, that where a man can live,
there he can also **live well**.
- Marcus Aurelius

Bad habits are like **chains** that are too light to feel
until they are too heavy to carry.
- Warren Buffett

The nature of man is always the same; it is their habits that separate them.
- Confucius

We're worn into grooves by Time – by our **habits**.
In the end, these grooves are going to show whether
we've been second rate or **champions**.
- Frank B. Gilbreth

We are ruled by our **habits**. When habits are young they are like lion cubs, soft, fluffy, funny, frolicsome little animals.

They grow day by day. Eventually they **rule you**.
Choose ye this day the habit ye would have to rule over you.
— Elbert Hubbard

The **most valuable** of all education is the ability to make yourself do the thing you have to do when it has to be done, whether you **like it** or not.
— Aldous Huxley

We must make automatic and habitual, as early as possible, as many useful **actions** as we can. The more of the details of our daily life we can hand over to the effortless custody of automation,
the more our higher **powers of mind** will be set free for their own proper work.
— William James

Failure is only postponed success as long as courage coaches ambition.
The habit of persistence is the habit of victory.
— Herbert Kaufman

The beginning of a habit is like an **invisible thread**, but every time we repeat the act we strengthen the strand, add to it another filament,
until it becomes a **great cable** and binds us irrevocably.
— Orison Swett Marden

It is just as easy to form a **good habit** as it is a bad one. And it is just as hard to break a good habit as a bad one. So get the good ones and **keep them**.
- *William McKinley*

The man who succeeds above his fellows is the one who early in life clearly discerns his object, and towards that object habitually directs his powers.
- *Earl Nightingale*

Man is a bundle of habits; in a word,
there is not a **quality or function**, either of body or mind,
which does not feel the influence of this great law of animated nature.
- *William Paley*

If you are going to achieve **excellence** in big things,
you develop the habit in little matters.
Excellence is not an exception, it is a prevailing **attitude**.
- *Colin Powell*

Sow an act and you reap a **habit**.
Sow a habit and you reap a **character**.
Sow a character and you reap a **destiny**.
- *Charles Reade*

Incredibly, many people continue their old life-style,
their **habits**, even if they feel miserable, lonely, bored, inadequate, or abused.
Why? Of course... because habit is an easy **place to hide**.
- *Tom Rusk*

Motivation is what gets you started. Habit is what keeps you going.
- *Jim Ryun*

When you do the wrong thing, knowing it is wrong, you do so because you
haven't developed the habit of **effectively controlling** or neutralizing
strong inner urges that tempt you, or because you have established the wrong
habits and don't know how to eliminate them effectively.
- *W. Clement Stone*

The formation of right habits is **essential** to your permanent security.
- *John Tyndall*

Habits are about the only servants that will work for you for nothing.
Just get them established,
and they will **operate** even though you are going around in a trance.
- *Frederic Whitaker*

I have learned that success is to be measured not
so much by the position that one has reached in life
as by the obstacles that one has overcome
while trying to succeed.

- Booker T. Washington

Roadblocks? Go Around Them!

*B*orn in Maryland to a slave woman early in the 19th century, Frederick Bailey never knew his father's identity. As a baby, he was taken from his mother and saw her only briefly until her death when he was about seven. Even at that age, he was forced to work as a slave, suffered frequent beatings, and endured long hours without food or sleep. Later, he would write: "I was broken in body, soul and spirit."

The one bright spot in his bleak existence came when his owner's wife taught him to read and write. That act of kindness would become the catalyst that would eventually allow Frederick to overcome the enormous obstacles placed in his path and bring him success and fame.

As a young man, he escaped, and made his way to New York and then to New England. He became active in the abolitionist movement and was encouraged to publicly share his story of his life as a slave. He was a brilliant speaker, and the publication of his autobiography, while still in his thirties, made him world famous. He later spent two years on a lecture tour of Great Britain and Ireland.

After returning to the U.S., he met with President Abraham Lincoln to discuss plans to free the slaves. He became a successful newspaper publisher, editor, author and public speaker. In 1888, at the Republican National Convention, he became the first African-American to receive a vote for President of the United States.

At the time of his death in 1895, Frederick, who as a young man had changed his last name to Douglass, had overcome obstacles few of us would ever have to face and became one of the most prominent and successful figures in U.S. and African-American history.

When you come to a roadblock, **take a detour**.
- Mary Kay Ash

If you trust in God and yourself, you can **surmount** every obstacle.
Do not yield to restless anxiety.
One must not always be asking what may happen to one in life,
but one must advance, **fearlessly** and **bravely**.
- Otto von Bismarck

Wanting something is not enough. You must **hunger** for it.
Your motivation must be **absolutely compelling** in order to overcome the
obstacles that will invariably come your way.
- Les Brown

The block of granite which was an obstacle in the pathway of the weak
becomes a stepping-stone in the pathway of the strong.
- Thomas Carlyle

Out of suffering have emerged the **strongest souls**;
the most massive characters are seared with scars.
- Edwin H. Chapin

Ride on! Rough-shod if need be, smooth-shod if that will do, but **ride on**!
Ride on over all obstacles, and **win** the race.
- Charles Dickens

All the adversity I've had in my life,
all my troubles and obstacles, have strengthened me...
You may not realize it when it happens,
but a kick in the teeth may be the best thing in the world for you.
- Walt Disney

Obstacles are the muscles of **achievement**.
- Ella E. Dodson

It is a hard **rule of life**, and I believe a healthy one,
that no great plan is ever carried out without meeting and overcoming
endless obstacles that come up to try the skill of man's hand,
the quality of his **courage**, and the endurance of his **faith**.
- Donald Douglas

Adversity toughens manhood,
and the characteristic of the good or the great man,
is not that he has been exempted from the evils of life,
but that he has surmounted them.
- Patrick Henry

It still holds true that man is most uniquely human
when he turns **obstacles into opportunities**.
- Eric Hoffer

If you're trying to achieve, there **will be** roadblocks.
I've had them; everybody has had them.
But obstacles don't have to stop you.
If you run into a wall, don't turn around and give up.
Figure out how to **climb it**, go **through it**, or work **around it**.
- Michael Jordan

Obstacles cannot crush me.
Every obstacle yields to **stern resolve**.
He who is fixed to a star does not change his mind.
- Leonardo da Vinci

We find no real satisfaction or happiness in life
without obstacles to conquer and goals to achieve.
- Maxwell Maltz

The person who has not struggled with difficulty after difficulty cannot know the
joy of **genuine success**. Face the problems and fight your way over them...
The rungs in the ladder of success are composed of **difficulties**.
- Vern McLellan

The majority see the obstacles;
the few see the objectives;
history rewards the **successes** of the latter,
while oblivion is the reward of the former.
- Alfred A. Montapert

Obstacles are those frightful things you see
when you take your eyes off **the goal**.
- Hannah More

No tree becomes **rooted** and **sturdy** unless many a wind assails it.
For by its very tossing it tightens its grip and plants its roots more securely.
- Seneca the Younger

Life's up and downs provide windows of **opportunity**
to determine your values and goals.
Think of using all obstacles as **stepping stones** to build the life you want.
- Marsha Sinetar

Adversity causes some men to break; others to break records.
- William A. Ward

Failure should be our teacher,
not our undertaker.
Failure is delay, not defeat.
It is a temporary detour,
not a dead-end street.

- William Arthur Ward

Never Let Failure Stop You

Augustine's mom had big dreams for her son. "You're going to be a great writer," she kept telling him. By age five, he was reading adult books and, while he was in high school, his goal was to attend college and study Journalism.

Then, when he was 17, his mother died and the dream seemed ended. He joined the U.S. Army Air Corps, flying 30 combat missions during World War II.

After the war, he tried to find work but, "there wasn't a big demand for bombardiers with a high school education." He married his high school sweetheart and became a life insurance salesman. After work, he began stopping at a bar, "for one drink," which soon became many. Then his wife left him, taking their young daughter, and he lost his house and his job.

"I was a drunk," he said, "a 35-year-old bum, ready to end it all. I had thirty dollars in my pocket, and when I saw a gun in a pawnshop for twenty-nine dollars, I almost bought it."

Instead, at a local library, he began reading a motivational book, and was so impressed that he contacted the author, who hired him as a salesman. After writing a sales manual, he became sales manager and later editor of his company's motivational magazine, where he remained until the first of his eighteen books was published.

That long-ago dream of his mother's finally came true, to a far greater degree than either of them could have imagined. Along the way, he began using a shortened version of his given name, or Aug, which, on a whim one day, he decided to spell as Og.

By the time he died in 1996, Og Mandino had become the most widely read inspirational author in the world, with sales of more than fifty million copies of his books in twenty-five languages. For all of us who, at some point in our lives have known disappointment and failure, he left this advice: "Remind thyself, in the darkest moments, that every failure is only a step toward success."

I have always felt that although someone **may** defeat me,
and I strike out in a ball game,
the pitcher on the particular day was the best player.
But I know when I see him again,
I'm going to **be ready** for his curve ball.
Failure is a part of success.
- Hank Aaron

We mount to heaven mostly on the ruins of our cherished schemes,
finding our failures were **successes**.
- Amos Bronson Alcott

Those who try and fail are much wiser than those who never try for fear of failure.
- André Bustanoby

Failure is the condiment that gives **success** its flavor.
- Truman Capote

Beware of succumbing to failure as inevitable;
make it the **stepping-stone** to success.
- Oswald Chambers

Failure is **instructive**.
The person who really thinks learns quite as much
from his failures as from his successes.
- *John Dewey*

I have not failed. I've just found 10,000 ways that won't work.
- *Thomas A. Edison*

Most of us know that the **joy** of anticipated success
can turn to ashes in the day of failure.
Yet, **success** is only possible if the potential for failure exists.
- *Ted W. Engstrom*

Failure doesn't consist in stumbling and falling.
The failure is **staying** there on the floor.
Success is finding something while you're down there to pick up with you.
- *James S. Hewett*

Failure: Often that early morning hour of darkness
which precedes the dawning of the **day of success**.
- *Leigh Mitchell Hodges*

Failure is often God's own tool for carving some of the finest outlines
in the **character** of His children; and, even in this life, bitter and crushing
failures have often in them the germs of new and quite **unimagined happiness**.
- Thomas Hodgkin

Albeit failure in any cause produces a correspondent misery in the soul, yet it
is, in a sense, the **highway to success**, in as much as every **discovery** of
what is false leads us to seek earnestly after what is true.
- John Keats

**Failures, repeated failures, are finger posts on the road to achievement.
One fails forward toward success.**
- Charles F. Kettering

He who hopes to avoid all failure and misfortune is trying to live in a **fairyland**;
the wise man readily accepts failures as a part of life
and builds a philosophy to **meet them** and **make the most** of them.
- Wilfred A. Peterson

Nothing succeeds like failure. We **learn** far more about ourselves in our failures
than in our successes. Failure is the **greatest teacher** of all.
Failure dramatizes where we are yet incomplete, and points the way to wholeness.
So failure may be the future signaling to us.
- Robert A. Raines

Far better it is to dare mighty things,
to win **glorious** triumphs,
even though checkered by failure,
than to take rank with those poor spirits who neither enjoy much nor suffer much,
because they live in the gray twilight that knows neither **victory nor defeat**.
- Theodore Roosevelt

You always pass failure on the way to success.
- Mickey Rooney

It is a mistake to suppose that men succeed through success;
they much oftener **succeed through failures**.
Precept, study, advice, and example could never have taught them
so well as failure has done.
- Samuel Smiles

Failure is as much a part of life as **success** is
and by no means something in front of which one sits down
and howls as though it is a scandal and a shame.
- J. Neville Ward

Every failure is a step to success;
every detection of what is false directs us toward what is true;
every trial exhausts some tempting form of error.
- William Whewell

You need to be aware of what others are doing, applaud their efforts, acknowledge their successes, and encourage them in their pursuits. When we all help one another, everybody wins.

- Jim Stovall

Encouragement: Oxygen for Your Soul

In 1913, James Cleveland Owens was born into a sharecropper's family in Alabama, and moved to Ohio when he was nine. Asked at school for his name, he gave his initials, J.C., which his teacher misunderstood as Jesse. And it was as Jesse Owens that he became a world-famous athlete in track, winning four gold medals in the 1936 Olympics and setting numerous world records during his career.

In his later years, Owens often spoke to young students, encouraging them as he had been encouraged as a boy. "The top athletes," he once said, "can keep the kids interested and out of trouble. They inspire kids, just as I was inspired by athletes when I was younger."

One athlete Owens often credited for encouraging him was Charlie Paddock, who had won several medals in the 1920 and 1924 Olympics. Later, Paddock spoke at Jesse's school, and the young boy was spellbound.

"You can be somebody," Paddock told his audience. "You can be anything you want to be if you have a goal and will work and believe and have good moral character." Years later, Jesse could still quote those words from memory, as a key to the enormous success he would achieve.

In 1970, he was inducted into the Alabama Sports Hall of Fame and, in 1976, President Gerald Ford honored him with the Presidential Medal of Freedom. Even after his death in 1980, honors continued to come in. President George H.W. Bush named him a recipient of a Congressional Gold Medal and, in 1996, the Jesse Owens Memorial Park opened in his hometown of Oakville, Alabama.

Inscribed on a bronze plaque in that park are these words:

May his light shine forever as a symbol for all who run for the freedom of sport, for the spirit of humanity, for the memory of Jesse Owens.

Note how good you feel after you have **encouraged** someone else.
No other argument is necessary to suggest that
you should never miss the **opportunity to give** encouragement.
- George Burton Adams

We should seize every opportunity to give encouragement.
Encouragement is oxygen to the soul.
The days are always dark enough.
There is not need for us to emphasize the fact by spreading further gloom.
- George Matthew Adams

There are high spots in all of our lives,
and most of them have come about through **encouragement** from someone else.
I don't care how great, how famous, or successful a man or woman may be,
each **hungers** for applause.
- George Matthew Adams

Encouragement is of constant need both in the inner world of **progress**
and in the outer world of **success**.
- Sri Chinmoy

Most of us, swimming against the tides of trouble the world knows nothing about,
need only a bit of **praise** or **encouragement** – and we will make the goal.
- Robert Collier

Correction does much, but **encouragement** does more.
Encouragement after censure is as the sun after a shower.
- Johann von Goethe

Those who are **lifting** the world **upward** and **onward**
are those who encourage more than criticize.
- Elizabeth Harrison

Abilities wither under faultfinding, **blossom** under encouragement.
- Donald A. Laird

Remember, man does not **live** on bread alone:
sometimes he **needs** a little buttering up.
- John C. Maxwell

A smile of encouragement at the right moment
may act like sunlight on a closed up flower;
it may be the turning point for a struggling life.
- Alfred A. Montapert

Encouragement is food for the **heart**, and every heart is a hungry heart.
- *Pat Morley*

It takes so little to make us glad,
Just a cheering clasp or a friendly hand,
Just a word from one who can understand;
And we finish the task we long had planned,
And we lose the doubt and fear we had
So little it takes to make us glad.
- *Ida Goldsmith Morris*

One of the most beautiful gifts in the world is the **gift of encouragement**.
When someone encourages you, that person helps you over a threshold you
might otherwise never have crossed on your own.
- *John O'Donohue*

People have a way of **becoming** what you encourage
them to be—not what you nag them to be.
- *Scudder N. Parker*

Words of encouragement fan the **spark** of genius into the **flame** of achievement.
- *Wilfred A. Peterson*

What men and women need is **encouragement**. Instead of always harping
on a man's faults, tell him of his **virtues**.
- *Eleanor H. Porter*

Three billion people go to bed hungry every night,
but four billion go to bed hungry for **a simple word** of encouragement.
- Cavett Robert

The way to develop the best that is in a man
is by **appreciation** and **encouragement**.
- Charles M. Schwab

Flatter me, and I may not believe you. Criticize me, and I may not like you.
Ignore me, and I may not forgive you. Encourage me, and I will not forget you.
- William Arthur Ward

A pat on the back is only a few vertebrae removed from
a kick in the pants, but is **miles ahead** in results.
- Ella Wheeler Wilcox

Encouragement is awesome.
Think about it: It has the capacity to **lift** a man's or woman's shoulders.
To **spark** the flicker of a smile on the face of a discouraged child.
To **breathe** fresh fire into the fading embers of a smoldering dream.
- Charles Swindoll

Always remember there are two types of people in the world. Those who come into a room and say, "Well, here I am!" and those who come in and say, "Ah, there you are!"

- Frederick L. Collins

Spread Sunshine into Other Lives

*I*n 1865, an itinerant preacher who had been walking the streets of London for more than a decade held a series of meetings in a tent set up in a London churchyard. That was the beginning of a movement that would spread rapidly, first throughout the British Isles, and on to the U.S., France, India, South Africa, Argentina, Zimbabwe and some two dozen other nations, all by the end of the 19th century. Today, The Salvation Army is one of the largest and most widely respected charitable organizations in the world.

What has been the key to its enormous and long-lasting success? The answer can be found in a single word, expressed by its founder, General William Booth, more than a century ago. One year, with his troops spread around the world, he wanted to send them a Christmas greeting, encouraging them to continue to serve a hurting world. At that time, the only means of rapid communication was via telegram, an expensive process, with fees based on the number of words used.

The general was a practical and frugal man, and found a single word to convey his message. A single word – but it spoke volumes. His telegram read, simply: "Others."

However we define it, becoming successful is rarely, if ever, an individual achievement. As George Matthew Adams, an American author and columnist of a century ago, reminded us: "There is no such thing as a 'self-made' man. We are made up of thousands of others. Every one who has ever done a kind deed for us, or spoken one word of encouragement to us, has entered into the make-up of our character and of our thoughts, as well as our success."

Are we our "Brother's Keeper"?
We certainly are!
If we had no regard for others' **feelings** or **fortune**,
we would grow cold and indifferent to life itself.
Bound up with selfishness, we could not hope
for the success that could easily be ours.
- George Matthew Adams

Pretend that every single person you meet has a sign around his or her neck that says,
"**Make me feel important**."
Not only will you succeed in sales, you will **succeed** in life.
- Mary Kay Ash

Those who bring **sunshine** into the lives of others cannot keep it from themselves.
- James M. Barrie

A successful man is one who can't count the number of other successful people he helped to the top.
- Orlando A. Battista

The most attractive people in the world
are the ones who are interested in others –
turned outward in **cheerfulness**, **kindness**, **appreciation**,
instead of turned inward to be constantly centered in themselves.
- Pat Boone

The happiest people are rarely the richest, or the most beautiful, or even the most talented... Their eyes are turned outward; they are aware, compassionate. They have the capacity to love.
- *Jane Canfield*

An effort made for the **happiness** of others lifts us above ourselves.
- *Lydia Maria Child*

True success is the only thing that you cannot have unless and until you have **offered** it to others.
- *Sri Chinmoy*

It is one of the most **beautiful compensations** of this life that no man can sincerely try to help another without helping himself.
- *Ralph Waldo Emerson*

If there is any great secret of **success in life**, it lies in the ability to put yourself in the other person's place and to see things from his point of view – as well as your own.
- *Henry Ford*

It is literally true that you can succeed **best** and **quickest**
by helping others to succeed.
- Napoleon Hill

The secret of many a man's success in the world resides in **his insight**
into the moods of men, and **his tact** in dealing with them.
- J.G. Holland

There is no exercise better for the heart than
reaching down and **lifting** people up.
- John Andrew Holmes

Remember that there is no happiness in having or in getting, but only in giving.
Reach out. Share. Smile. Hug. Happiness is a perfume you cannot pour on others
without getting a few drops on yourself.
- Og Mandino

None of us has gotten where we are solely by pulling ourselves up by our own
bootstraps. We got here because somebody bent down and **helped us**.
- Thurgood Marshall

The most important single ingredient in the **formula of success**
is knowing how to get along with people.
- *Theodore Roosevelt*

I believe that the first test of a truly great man is his humility.
Really great men have a curious feeling
that the greatness is not in them but through them.
And they see something divine in every other man and are endlessly,
incredibly merciful.
- *John Ruskin*

Carve your name on **hearts** and not on marble.
- *Charles H. Spurgeon*

We cannot hold a **torch** to light another's path without **brightening** our own.
- *Ben Sweetland*

Success has nothing to do with what you **gain** in life or **accomplish** for yourself.
It's what you do for others.
- *Danny Thomas*

Man is much like a hole: the more you take away from him the bigger he gets. Greatness is always in terms of giving, not getting.

- Richard C. Halverson

Give Yourself Away

*H*e was born in Atlantic City, New Jersey, in 1932, and was adopted shortly thereafter. His family moved often and, at age 12, he got his first job, in a Knoxville, Tennessee restaurant. At 15, he was working as a busboy in a Fort Wayne, Indiana restaurant when his family decided to move again. Instead, he dropped out of high school to work full-time at the restaurant.

After serving in the U.S. Army during the Korean War, he went to work for Kentucky Fried Chicken in Columbus, Ohio, but later quit in order to pursue his dream of owning a hamburger restaurant. In 1969, the dream became reality when high school dropout Dave Thomas opened his first Wendy's Restaurant, named after his young daughter. Under his leadership, Wendy's grew to become the nation's third-largest fast-food chain specializing in burgers. At the time of his death in 2002, the number of Wendy's Restaurants had grown to more than 6,000.

Dave Thomas was a highly successful businessman, and a generous one as well. As a child, he spent several summers with his grandmother, who instilled in him the importance of always giving something back. During his career, he donated millions to dollars to various causes, including children's homes, hospitals and various charitable organizations. He lived the "giving back" lessons of his grandmother, saying: "Giving back doesn't simply mean giving money to charities. It also means giving your time or sharing your special skills."

Adoption causes were always close to his heart and, in 1992, he launched the Dave Thomas Foundation for Adoption, which continues to place thousands of children with adoptive parents. His generous spirit lives on, a glowing example of these words of 19th century poet Henry Wadsworth Longfellow:

> Lives of great men all remind us,
> We can make our lives sublime.
> And, departing, leave behind us
> Footprints on the sands of time.

That's what I consider **true generosity**.
You give your all and yet you always feel as if it costs you nothing.
- Simone de Beauvoir

We all have something to **give**.
So if you know how to read, find someone who can't.
If you've got a hammer, find a nail.
If you're not hungry, not lonely, not in trouble—seek out someone who is.
- George H.W. Bush

You can **give** without loving, but you cannot **love** without giving.
- Amy Carmichael

Real generosity is doing something nice for someone who will never find it out.
- Frank A. Clark

God sees the **heart**, not the hand; the **giver**, not the gift.
- Benjamin R. De Jong

Success is finding, or making, that position which enables you to **contribute**
to the world the very greatest services of which you are capable…
Success consists of **being** and **doing**, not simply accumulating.
- B.C. Forbes

The fragrance always remains on the hand that gives the rose.
- Mohandas K. Gandhi

You give but little when you give of your **possessions**.
It is when you give of **yourself** that you truly give.
- Kahlil Gibran

Complete possession is proved only by **giving**.
All you are unable to give possesses you.
- André Gide

There is no happiness in having and getting, but only in **giving**.
Half the world is on the wrong scent in the **pursuit of happiness**.
- Frank Wakely Gunsaulus

The manner of giving shows the character of the giver more than the gift itself.
- Johann K. Lavater

To give without any reward, or any notice, has **a special quality** of its own.
- Anne Morrow Lindbergh

The **greatest grace** of a gift, perhaps,
is that it anticipates and admits of no return.
- Henry Wadsworth Longfellow

The way to happiness:
Keep your **heart** free from hate,
your **mind** from worry.
Live simply,
expect **little**,
give much.
Scatter **sunshine**.
Forget self,
think of **others**.
- Norman Vincent Peale

We must teach our children that what is ours in life is only in **trust**,
to be given to worthy causes—
and what man has in life he keeps only that which is given away.
- James Cash Penney

If there be any truer measure of a man than by what he **does**,
it must be by what he **gives**.
- Robert South

The less I spent on myself and the more I gave to others,
the fuller of happiness and blessing did my soul become.
- Hudson Taylor

Don't be reluctant to give of yourself **generously**;
it's the mark of **caring** and **compassion** and **personal greatness**.
- Brian Tracy

It is not the shilling I give you that counts,
but the **warmth** that it carries with it from my hand.
- Miguel de Unamuno

I have usually proceeded on the principle that persons who **possess sense**
enough to earn money have sense enough to know how to give it away.
- Booker T. Washington

Four short words
sum up what has lifted
most successful individuals
above the crowd:
a little bit more.
They did all that was expected
of them and a little bit more.

— A. Lou Vickery

Go the Extra Mile

*I*n the Introduction to her book, *My Father's Hand: A Daughter's Reflection on a Father's Wisdom*, professional speaker Naomi Rhode shares a story her father often told: "Having lived through the Great Depression... my Dad had a true appreciation of thrift. But far beyond thrift was a philosophy of giving. He'd often tell the story of the shopkeeper during the Great Depression:

> 'This shopkeeper was different than all the other shopkeepers in town. When you came into his shop to buy five pounds of coffee beans, he would take his marvelous scale and put a five-pound weight on one side, and the empty container on the other. Then, he would ceremoniously put the scoop into the bag of freshly roasted coffee beans, scooping and scooping until the once empty container was perfectly balanced with the five-pound weight.

> 'The shopkeeper would then pause – and "twinkle" – and dip the scoop into the bag of beans one more time. With a smile, he would empty that extra scoop of coffee beans on top of what he had so carefully measured, overflowing the container and tipping the scales in favor of you, the customer.

> 'As he smiled and twinkled, he would say "Lagniappe," which in French Creole means: "every bit you paid for, and then just a little bit extra." It was obviously that "little bit extra" which had created, built and successfully retained the business other shops lost during that difficult time in our nation's history.'"

Giving that little bit extra, going the extra mile, making that final effort – those are the things that pay dividends, that bring success.

No student ever attains very eminent success by simply doing what is required of him: it is the amount and excellence of what is **over** and **above** the required that determines the greatness of **ultimate distinction**.
- Charles Kendall Adams

Go that extra mile that failures refuse to travel.
It is far better to be exhausted from **success** than to be rested from failure.
- Mary Kay Ash

The real tragedy is the tragedy of the man who never in his life braces himself for his one supreme effort, who never stretches to his full capacity, never stands up to his full stature.
- Arnold Bennett

There is a lot of pleasure in doing more than you have to.
"And whosoever shall compel you to go a mile, **go with him** twain,"
says the Bible, wisely.
- Norman Carlisle

Do your duty and a **little bit more**, and the future will take care of itself.
- Andrew Carnegie

The only way of discovering the limits of the **possible**
is to venture **a little way past** them into the impossible.
- Arthur C. Clarke

Whenever we do what we can, we immediately can **do more**.
- James Freeman Clarke

If you want to become the greatest in your field, no matter what it may be,
equip yourself to render **greater service** than anyone else.
- Clinton Davidson

As memory scans the past, above and beyond all the transitory pleasures of life,
there leap forward those supreme hours when you have been enabled to do unnoticed
kindnesses to those round about you, things too trifling to speak about.
- Henry Drummond

The successful person is only **a little bit better** than the one who fails.
- Ted W. Engstrom

The man who will use his skill and **constructive imagination**
to see how much he can give for a dollar,
instead of how little he can give for a dollar, is **bound to succeed**.
- Henry Ford

Start by doing what's **necessary**;
then do what's **possible**;
and suddenly you are doing the **impossible**.
- Saint Francis of Assisi

**Victory is not won in miles but in inches.
Win a little now, hold your ground, and later win a little bit more.**
- Louis L'Amour

The **victory of success** will be half won when you learn the secret
of putting out more than is expected in all that you do...
Exercise your privilege to go the ***extra mile***, and enjoy all the rewards you receive.
- Og Mandino

The only certain means is to render **more** and **better** service than is expected of you,
no matter what your task may be.
- Og Mandino

Do a **little bit more** than average and from that point on
our progress multiplies itself out of all proportion to the effort put in.
- Paul J. Meyer

There are no traffic jams along **the extra mile**.
- Roger Staubach

Do a little **more** each day than you think you possibly can.
- Lowell Thomas

Success is to be measured not by wealth, power, or fame,
but by the ratio between what a man is and what he might be.
- H.G. Wells

BOB KELLY

Bob Kelly began his freelance writing career at age 15, covering high school sports events for The New York Times (at $5 per event). After graduation from college with a degree in Journalism and English, he spent many years as a commercial banker before returning to his first love.

In 1979, he founded WordCrafters, Inc., offering a wide range of editorial services, including newsletters, direct mail and ghostwriting. From 1982 to 1988, he was also editor and publisher of the Pasadena Journal of Business and a freelance writer for other business newspapers.

During his career, he has authored or co-authored 18 books, including pictorial histories of such well-known communities as Los Angeles, Beverly Hills, Pasadena (twice), Santa Monica and Colorado Springs. He has also ghostwritten numerous books on business, financial and professional topics.

In 1982, he began building a library of quotations, which now numbers 425 published volumes, many of them dating back to the 19th century. His collection encompasses more than one-and-a-half million selections, perhaps the largest in the English-speaking world.

He has edited and compiled several volumes of quotations, including In Celebration of Children; Worth Repeating: More than 5,000 Classic and Contemporary Quotes; and The Tremendous Power of Prayer. The last named, on which he collaborated with the late well-known motivational speaker, Charlie "Tremendous" Jones, received a Silver Angel Award in 2001 from Hollywood-based Excellence in Media.

Since 2003, Bob has been writing and publishing a free monthly online newsletter, titled The KellyGram: Wit and Wisdom About the Wonderful and Often Wacky World of Words. Subscription information and back issues are available on his web site: www.wordcrafters.info.

MAC ANDERSON

Mac Anderson is the founder of Simple Truths and Successories, Inc., the leader in designing and marketing products for motivation and recognition. These companies, however, are not the first success stories for Mac. He was also the founder and CEO of McCord Travel, the largest travel company in the Midwest, and part owner/VP of sales and marketing for Orval Kent Food Company, the country's largest manufacturer of prepared salads.

His accomplishments in these unrelated industries provide some insight into his passion and leadership skills. He also brings the same passion to his speaking where he speaks to many corporate audiences on a variety of topics, including leadership, motivation, and team building.

Mac has authored or co-authored thirteen books that have sold over three million copies. His titles include:

> *212°: The Extra Degree*

> *Charging the Human Battery*

> *Customer Love*

> *Change is Good … You Go First*

> *Finding Joy*

> *Learning to Dance in the Rain*

> *Motivational Quotes*

> *The Dash*

> *The Essence of Leadership*

> *The Nature of Success*

> *The Power of Attitude*

> *To a Child, Love is Spelled T-I-M-E*

> *You Can't Send a Duck to Eagle School*

For more information about Mac, visit www.simpletruths.com